ANXIETY IN RELATIONSHIP

7 BOOKS IN 1
THE COMPLETE GUIDE TO OVERCOMING
INSECURITY, JEALOUSY AND NEGATIVE
THINKING. THERAPY TECHNIQUES TO STOP
FEELING INSECURE AND ATTACHED IN LOVE

Table of Contents

Introduction

What Is Anxiety?

Anxiety refers to the emotional state of being worried or afraid. As an emotion, anxiousness lies in the primary spectrum of emotions, including happiness, sadness, disappointment, etc. This emotion will be associated in some people's minds with a furrowed brow and worried facial expression; these are representing the state of heightened awareness that essentially serves as a hallmark for anxiousness.

There is also the condition of general anxiety disorder, which takes the primary anxiety that anyone can experience and describes a disease characterized by a prolonged period of anxious thoughts or worries that cause dysfunction in the impacted individual's life. Anxiety is, therefore, not dissimilar to depression in that it can characterize both a state and a disorder associated with a prolonged period in an anxious state. Although anxiousness is associated with fear, this feeling is generally regarded as an excessive state of worry, or as a fear that occurs dysfunctional, or in circumstances in which a person would not typically experience fear.

Are There Different Types of Anxiety?

Psychiatrists and medical professionals have described anxiety disorders to encapsulate the different forms that worry can take. Anxiousness is associated with excessive worries or fears, but the triggers for those worries or fears can vary. Generalized anxiety disorder (GAD) is characterized by excessive worries about various things or situations without an exact trigger. GAD distinct from other conditions that have a discrete trigger.

The Diagnostic and Statistical Manual defines several conditions as characterized by anxiety. However, some conditions have recently been separated from the anxiety disorder moniker and have been given their classifications. Several conditions are covered in addition to GAD. These include social anxiety disorder (social phobia), specific phobias, obsessive-compulsive disorder (OCD), post-traumatic stress disorder, situational anxiety, and panic disorder.

How Can Anxiety Impact a Relationship?

Worry can have a severe impact on a relationship. Anxious people may demonstrate excessive fear or physical symptoms that may render interacting with them difficult for people who may be unfamiliar with their condition. Anxious people also may avoid situations that can set off their disorder. This is true of people with GAD, social phobia, specific phobias, agoraphobia, post-traumatic stress disorder, and other conditions that fall under the spectrum of worry.

Although many people perceive anxiousness as being perhaps not as severely dysfunctional as other forms of mental illness (in part because anxiety is so common), anxiety remains a severe condition that can cause significant dysfunction in the lives of people suffering from these conditions. Someone with obsessive-compulsive disorder, for example, may find themselves trapped in behavior or obsessions and compulsions that renders it difficult for them to hold a job, leave the house, or have prolonged interactions with other people.

What Causes Anxiety?

The exact cause is not clear. This is an area of active debate. It has been observed that anxiousness is more common in Western countries than in the developed world. It also has been observed that anxious symptoms are more common in females than in males. An interesting observation regarding this condition is that as groups begin to adopt external features of Westernization, anxious conditions and other mental illness forms appear to become more common.

Of course, no one can say why anxiety happens or why it seems to impact some groups more than others. Anxiousness does appear to have a genetic component, although not all cases can be accounted for by genetics. In other words, anxiousness does tend to run in families, although some individuals may develop an anxiety disorder even though no one in their family has experienced worry. Another area of study is the role that the media plays in this condition, although this is a subject that is a long way away from concluding.

How Is Anxiety Treated?

As with other mental health conditions, anxiety can be treated in several different ways. Treatment can generally be divided into three categories. These categories include therapy and behavior modification, medication, and alternative medicine. Anxiety disorders are unique. Although medication is an essential aspect of treatment, many medication treatments for anxious conditions were not designed to treat these disorders, but others, especially depression. Indeed, antidepressant medications are among the most common treatments for anxiety. SSRIs and SNRIs (types of antidepressants) are very popular in the treatment of anxiety. As depression represents significant comorbidity shared with anxiousness, psychiatrists often find antidepressants almost a panacea for their patients who suffer from anxiousness and depression.

How common Is Anxiety?

Anxiety is pervasive. A rough estimate that nearly one in ten people suffer from it in a given year. This number is believed to be higher in Western countries like the United States. Although many people may think of generalized anxiety disorder when they hear the word anxiety, GAD represents less than half of the anxiety cases, or so the psychiatric community believes. Other conditions like specific phobias, social phobia, and situational anxiety account for much of the experienced anxiety experienced worldwide.

How Is Anxiety related to Depression? Why Are Antidepressant Medications Prescribed for Anxiety?

Anxiety and depression can frequently co-occur. Indeed, it has been found that a large percentage of people that are diagnosed with major depressive disorder also have an anxiety disorder of some kind. Although it is not clear why these conditions tend to overlap, there is an aspect of brain chemistry dysfunction that appears to be shared between anxiety and depression.

Neurotransmitters are the brain's molecules to communicate across the central nervous system (CNS). Neurotransmitters are released from one end of the synapse bond to their receptor sites at the other end of the synapse, triggering a message carried across the neurons to their target areas. Many psychiatric medications work by modifying concentrations of neurotransmitters at the synapse, which is true of medications that treat depression and anxiety. In particular, antidepressants commonly increase concentrations of serotonin, norepinephrine, or dopamine at the synapse, suggesting that these neurotransmitters are essential in the signaling pathways related to depression and fear.

Is There Stigma surrounding Anxiety?

There is a stigma surrounding many mental health conditions, including anxiety. Although one might imagine that common conditions like anxiety or depression would be associated with less stigma than others, there is still a significant stigma regarding these conditions. Sometimes the stigma can take the shape of a loved one disregarding depressive or anxious symptoms because of their own subjective experiences with these conditions. Others may feel that depression and anxiety are problems that everyone faces and can be resolved without any significant intervention.

Are Partners of Anxious Persons at Risk for Developing Anxiety Themselves?

There is the phenomenon of the partners of depressed people becoming depressed themselves. Although this has not been observed as frequently in anxious people, it is a development that some individuals in the mental health community warn others to be cautious about. This finding that anxious people can become anxious is perhaps related to the comorbidity between anxiety and depression. In other words, the worry that develops in both partners can be depression that also develops an anxiety disorder component. But considering how heterogeneous anxiety disorders can be in their presentation, it cannot be said with certainty that anxiety that develops in two partners in a couple is not an anxious condition but depression.

Part One:

Anxious in Love

CHAPTER 1:

Understanding Your Anxiety

Falling and being in love challenges us in various and numerous ways. A number of these challenges are unexpected, and when we face them the first time, our human nature makes us defensive.

That defensive tension becomes a barrier. This feeling may also arise because of our perception. The things you tell yourself about a relationship, love, attraction, desire, et cetera will affect our lives. This means that you might have the best partner in the world, but your thoughts still hinder you from realizing it and enjoying the moment. The proverbial 'Inner voice' is very dangerous if it is negative. This mental couch can tell us things that fuel our fear of intimacy. The critical inner voice can feed us lousy advice such as "You are too ugly for him/her," "Even the other people have left you before," "You cannot trust such a man/woman."

What do such thoughts do? They make us turn against the people we love and, most importantly, ourselves. The critical inner voice can make us hostile, paranoid, and unnecessarily suspicious. It can also drive our feelings of defensiveness, distrust, anxiety, and jealousy to unhealthy levels. This tiny negative voice feeds us an endless stream of unhealthy thoughts that make us worried about relationships and undermine our happiness. It prevents us from enjoying life wholesomely.

The main challenge comes in once we focus on these thoughts. We get into our heads and focus on whatever that minute thought is saying. Then we process it and ponder it and roast and re-roast it until it appears like an unmovable mountain. At that moment, one is distracted from his/her partner; thus, no real relationship and interaction. After brewing over the thoughts, one might start to act out, either immaturely or in destructive ways. For instance, one might start to boss the partner around, monitoring all his/her moves, making unnecessary nasty comments, ignoring, or mistreating the other.

Supposing your partner stays late at work or passes by the local bar for a drink before coming home. The critical inner thought will trigger thoughts such as "where is he/she? What is he doing?" with who and why? Does she/he [prefer to be away from home? Maybe he/she doesn't love me anymore." In this state, it becomes hard to have a constructive conversation about his/her whereabouts.

Consequently, this partner will feel misunderstood and frustrated. Furthermore, he/she will also take a defensive stance. Soon, the dynamic of the relationship shifts from pleasure and comfort to irrational and unfair treatments.

Do you realize that in such a case, you have effectively created the distance you initially feared? O you also realize that your partner might have had no harmful intentions. The fact is, the distance you have created was not caused by the situation itself or circumstances. No. It was triggered by that critical inner voice, which might have been wrong. That voice colored your thinking with negativity, distorted your perception, and, in the end, led you to self-destruction.

The biggest challenge that leads us to self-destruction in relationships is self-doubt. If we assess most of the things we worry about in a relationship, we realize that we can handle the consequences. The majority of us are resilient enough to experience heartbreaks and heal. It probably has happened before, and you did not die from it. However, our inner voice tends to blow things out of proportion, especially the negative ones. That voice terrorizes and catastrophizes everything making it hard to stay rational. It can trigger severe anxiety spells over some non-existent relationship dynamics that do not exist and strange, intangible threats.

Probably, break-ups would not be so painful if we did not have that critical voice. It is the thing that analyses things and tears us apart by pointing out all our flaws and things we failed to do. The distorted reality makes us think that we are not healthy and resilient enough to survive. That critical voice is the cynical friend who is always giving bad advice "You cannot survive a heartbreak, just stay guarded and do not become vulnerable."

We form our defenses depending on unique life experiences and adaptations. The inner voice also borrows from those unique experiences. If a former partner said that he/she would leave you because you are overweight or underweight, the inner voice would use that line to distort reality. It will make you think that another partner is noticing the same flaws and that he/she will leave because of them. When feeling insecure or anxious, some of us tend to become desperate or clingy in our actions. Others become control freaks, wanting to possess the partner. Many people start to feel crowded, like there is no breathing space in the relationship, thus choosing to distance themselves from their loved ones. In extreme cases, we detach from the feelings of desire in their relationship. We can start to be aloof, guarded, or wholly withdrawn. Such patterns of attachment and relating can come from our early life experiences. In childhood years, we develop attachment patterns, unconsciously, depending on our environment. The patterns become the model for our adult life. They influence how we assess our needs and how we get them fulfilled. These attachment patterns and styles are the main determinants of anxiety one feels in a relationship. Understanding the difference between normal sensations of anxiety and an anxiety disorder calling for clinical attention can help individuals identify and treat the problem. Everybody feels distressed now and then. It's a normal emotion. For example, you may contact worried when faced with trouble at the office, before taking a test or making a vital choice.

Stress and anxiety conditions are different, though. They are a group of mental diseases, and the distress they trigger can maintain you from carrying on with your life regularly. For individuals who have one, worry and anxiety are constant and frustrating and can be disabling. However, with therapy, many individuals can take care of those sensations and get back to a satisfying life. When an individual encounters possibly harmful or distressing triggers, feelings of stress and anxiety are not just typical but necessary for survival.

CHAPTER 2:

Recognizing Your Anxiety Triggers

Unhealthy anxiety can have a significant impact on your life. It will hinder you from doing the things you desire. When you are anxious, you feel that your life is under the control of an external force. Anxiety is a negative, vicious circle that consumes you entirely and can affect your well-being, relationship, hobbies, and more. It feels challenging to break this anxiety, but the possibility exists. Anxiety often makes people assume that they are no longer in charge and cannot do anything about it. This isn't the case - you can learn to get your anxieties under control and find happiness.

Anxiety disorder occurs when you regularly feel disproportionate levels of worry, tension, or fear due to an emotional trigger. The ability to identify the reason behind a series of anxiety attacks is the key to successful treatment.

- **Environmental factors:** Elements within your surroundings can trigger anxiety. Worries and stress associated with a personal relationship, job, school, or monetary difficulty can lead to anxiety disorder.

- **Medical factors:** Different medical issues can lead to an anxiety disorder, such as the side effects of drugs, symptoms of a sickness, or stress from a problematic underlying medical condition. These conditions could lead to significant lifestyle changes like pain, restricted movement, and even emotional imbalance.

- **Brain chemistry:** Experiences traumatizing or stressful can alter the brain's structure and performance, making it react to specific triggers that may not have before caused anxiety.

Relationships are unique and very fulfilling with the opportunity for happiness, fun, interesting conversations, and exciting dates. They can, however, also be a significant source of upheaval and worry. Your ability to identify the significant sources of anxiety in your relationship will help you stay away from them, thus enhancing your relationship's balance and stability.

What triggers anxiety the most is when you are vulnerable to another person. We yearn for safety and love in a relationship. If you have been hurt before, the fear of being hurt again can make you anxious.

Financial concerns of either partner are another cause of anxiety in relationships. Most times, people do not fully disclose their money related issues or financial strengths. They open up when a problem arises, and at this point, it may be too late. When real-life expenses set in and you seem to be carrying the brunt of them, anxiety sets in. Money in relationships is a constant.

Another root cause of anxiety in relationships is jealousy. Your inability to trust your partner could lead to jealousy. Jealousy is also a result of a lack of confidence in yourself and your abilities coupled with low self-esteem. To overcome this, build up your self-esteem and begin to think very highly of yourself. The best way to eradicate jealousy is by building up your self-esteem.

Jealousy can reveal our greatest fears and insecurities, which can quickly lead to an unhealthy and toxic atmosphere in your relationship. When you are jealous, you become overwhelmed and begin to imagine the worst.

The fear of being abandoned and the fear of rejection are also significant causes of anxiety in relationships. Whatever insecurities you have are mirrored back to you by your partner. It is only normal to worry about these things, but instead of keeping the thoughts to yourself, speak them out loud and have a conversation about them with your partner. You have to develop a stronger identity and sense of self. You have to learn to be consciously aware of your state of mind and thought processes to keep all anxieties at bay. Most of the arguments you have with your partner over your family, work, social life, or money have some form of rejection as their roots.

Your ability to relax into your relationship will make you feel less rejected and no longer defensive. Be present in your relationship and have no negative thoughts.

You must deliberately set clear boundaries on the type of information that gets into your head. Work to stop unwanted information and behaviors from coming in and penetrating your mind.

When anxiety comes knocking at your door, open the door for it, address it, look at it, then inhale deeply and close the door, knowing that you have armed yourself with all the information that you need. You do not have to welcome anxiety with open arms, but you can acknowledge that it's there.

Ongoing communication with an ex is another trigger for anxiety. Communications with an ex should be handled cautiously. This is because it can lead to significant anxiety, anger, and, eventually, a break-up in your current relationship. If you do not have to communicate with your ex, do not do it.

Distance backed up with a lack of communication can hugely contribute to anxiety between you and your partner. When your partner is not physically available for an extended time, it can be challenging to find assurance, and thus, anxiety sets in. By so doing, your partner will be able to address this and reassure you of their love and commitment.

Another major cause of anxiety is a doubt. It can be weakening to question your partner's move and action, wondering if you made the right decision or what following steps you should or should not take. If you are in significant doubt, begin to make a conscious effort to release yourself and set yourself free from doubt. Take your mind off every question that makes you doubt your relationship or your partner. Just take a deep breath, calm down, and revel in your relationship.

CHAPTER 3:

Lowering Your Baseline Level of Anxiety

List Your Accomplishments

With the feelings of being unworthy, it is easy to lose sight of what you already have. Instead of drowning in a pool of self-pity, you should instead list down your accomplishments.

These are the things that you are proud to have achieved. Some of these things include your relationships, work, and even home. You don't necessarily need to have a million dollars in your bank account to feel like you have achieved something. All these matters have a positive attitude. When you list down your achievement, you will realize that you have accomplished many things.

Highlight Your Strengths

You lost your confidence due to having negative self-perception and thinking lowly of yourself. The truth is that everyone has their strong points. You just have to look hard enough.

Your strengths could be along the lines of the following qualities:

- Honesty
- Courage
- Friendliness
- Loyalty
- Self-discipline

Getting to look at the positive things about yourself will surely lift your self-esteem. You will start to look at yourself through the lens of positivity as opposed to negativity.

Set Goals

Low self-esteem may be brought about by a lack of direction in life. To remedy this, set goals for both the long-term and short-term, and it will surely increase both your determination and self-confidence. When you have an essential life goal to achieve, you are forced to stand up for what you believe in, and in the process, your self-confidence receives a significant boost. Self-confidence is not a spiritual thing that you can be bestowed. It is a quality of being that develops within you when you choose to step out of your comfort zone and challenge yourself.

Develop Your Assertiveness

You develop assertiveness by being conscious of your needs and choosing to stand for what you believe in. Start practicing your assertiveness with the ordinary people in your life. For instance, you go into a convenience store, and they get a tiny detail of your order wrong, don't ignore it. Ask them politely to get your order right. If you see someone that you want to talk to, don't hold yourself back. Walk up to them and express yourself. Developing your assertive skills is like growing your muscle.

Start Reading Manuscripts

When you read voraciously, you get to kick out ignorance and build up your self-esteem. In this age of the internet, it has even become easy to acquire reading materials. If you become an authority in a specific domain, you will attract people who will want to learn from you, which will naturally boost your self-confidence. An apparent cause of low self-esteem is ignorance. When you are ignorant about something, you're likely to react in a simple way, which guarantees a blow to your self-esteem. Read extensively – not just the manuscripts that will help you develop particular expertise.

Seek Out Confident Friends

We indeed become the average of the people we spend most of our time with. If we spend time with losers who are low on self-esteem, it follows that we will become just like them. Seeing that self-esteem takes practice, it is essential to have confident friends, because they will help you "talk the language of high self-esteem." For instance, your friends will help you give appropriate responses over many situations that you find yourself in.

28 | P a g .

Help Others

It's another secret of raising your self-esteem. Helping others, first of all, makes you feel good about yourself. Being altruistic will make you feel good about yourself, but more importantly, it will trigger a sense of self-worth in you. The more you view yourself in a great light, the more you increase your self-esteem. Helping others is also a way of expanding your network. Unless we are talking about someone who cannot do anything at all, but in most cases, when you help someone, they will go on to do amazing things with their life, and they will become an asset for you, not a liability.

Expand Your Social Circle

Developing excellent social skills is critical in boosting your self-esteem. We are social beings, we rely on social proof, and we need the input of others to fulfill our essential physical and psychological needs. The more adept you are at communicating with others, the more you strengthen your self-esteem — but you have to be careful in selecting the people you hang out with. Don't hang out with harmful elements of society.

Challenge Yourself

Another way of developing self-esteem is by challenging oneself. However, there's no real progress made in the comfort zone. However, if you take up a challenge, you will raise your standards and learn about character.

Perform the Things That You Are good at

We are all gifted differently. To achieve true happiness, we have to do something that we enjoy. We are also likely to have more confidence in ourselves when we take up challenges and activities that we enjoy doing.

.

CHAPTER 4:

Understanding Your Partner

Who are we as partners in the relationship? How do we step (literally and figuratively) towards and away from those on whom we depend? Like we have seen before, getting to know our ordinary people and ambassadors allows us in some way to address these questions. But in a relationship, not everyone can respond in the same way. Power balance varies from person to person inside and between primitive and ambassador camps. In reality, you and your partner can encounter various interactions between your primitive men and ambassadors due to your brain's variance.

Many partners are unaware of their relationships and how they connect in a married couple's environment. They try to show themselves in the best light, as in any audition. On the first day, it wouldn't make sense for anyone to say, "I have been alone as a child a lot of time, and I still am — I don't like being intruded in my time alone. Once I'm ready, I'll come to you. Don't get bothered to come to me because then I know you're asking me, and I don't like that. "An equally quick way to give a hill date would be to say," I just cling and get mad when I'm abandoned. I dislike and neglect silences. I do not seem to receive enough from people. Still, I don't get compliments well because I don't think people are genuine. I tend to reject something positive. "Partners may provide insights during the initial stage in a relationship about their necessary physical closeness preferences, personal privacy, and health and security concerns. Yet this preference comes to life only when the relationship is irreversible in one or both partners' minds.

Who Are You?

No one likes to be categorized, but it is mostly because we have minds that organize, sort, compare knowledge and experience by their very nature that we classify people and things around us. In reality, for centuries, people have described the human condition and still develop new ways of doing so —Scorpios or Capricorns, from Mars or Venus. We are liberals or libertarians, geeks, or Goths, atheists, or religious fanatics. Before we deplete or dehumanize anyone, those definitions will help us comprehend each other.

A significant aspect of this manual is that you identify your partner's interests and relationship types, explain and eventually mark them. It's much easier to work together and address problems when you know and appreciate each other's styles. It makes it easier to forgive and genuinely help because of the belief that "I know who you are." I'm not showing new or completely my designs. They are based on research findings first popularized almost half a century ago by John Bowlby (1969) and Mary Ainsworth and their fellow workers, who describe how babies develop an attachment.

First, don't try to push yourself if you don't figure out which style suits your partner best. The "mileage you get" from this information may vary. I presented these styles in their purest form. The vast majority knows one of the three types of people. In reality, people can be a mixture of different types, often making it hard to choose the most prominent. No worries, if that's the case to you. You should recall and use the one that best suits you in a particular situation. Second, my goal is to encourage reverence and empathy in discussing these types of what I believe are natural characteristics for human beings. Do not find them as flaws of character. Don't turn them into your partner's weapons. Alternatively, accept these types as the reasonable and necessary changes made by each of us in adulthood.

How We Develop Our Style of Relating?

As I said, we have a young age in our social wiring. It is how our parents or caregivers respond to us and to the world that decides whether we grow up to feel fundamentally safe or insecure. Parents who value relationships are more likely to defend their loved ones than parents who value other things. We prefer to spend more time with their children face-to-face and from skin to skin; be more curious and interested in their child's spirit, concentrate more closely, be more sensitive, and respond to their children's requirements. They build a healthy place for the child in this way.

CHAPTER 5:

Changing How You Handle Conflicts

Slamming doors, angry words, silent treatment, and a host of other destructive behaviors become the norm when fighting. Human beings are naturally emotional. Sadly, it is the people we love who hurt us the most. That is why, in every relationship, conflicts will arise.

The problem in a relationship is not that there is conflict but rather how the competition is handled. If you cannot resolve a disagreement without a shouting match or being mean to one another, you have an unhealthy way of resolving conflict.

It understands what kind of emotional reactions you are prone to when stressed or anxious can better control your emotions. This will help you to have disagreements without creating animosity or resorting to either aggressive or passive-aggressive behavior.

No matter how angry you feel, always remember the bigger picture. It may be gratifying to lash out at your partner in the heat of the moment, but how will your relationship be afterward? If every disagreement ended in a break-up, there would be no relationships to speak of.

Winning the Battle to Lose the War

Do you want to have a two-hour fight over who forgot to take out the trash? It is not unusual to find couples having blazing rows about the smallest of things. Constant bickering becomes a habit with time, and you start to see that the moments when you are in harmony with your partner become fewer each day. This is why it is essential to know how to pick your battles.

While you do not want to let your partner walks all over you, getting worked up over minor issues is self-sabotage. Living with a nagging partner can be emotionally draining and will, in most cases, drive the other person away. There is a reason some people will leave work and go straight to the bar instead of going home to their partners. There is nothing as important as peace of mind, and when you cannot get that at home, you start to seek it elsewhere.

Please resist the urge to start harping on them the minute they walk in through the door. When you know how to pick your moments, you will often get a better result because you do not aggravate or attack the other person.

Living in Harmony; the Basics Do's

I. It is okay to agree to disagree. Not every conflict has to end with both parties coming to the same agreement. On some issues, you will need to be okay with differing points of view.

II. Keep the personal attacks out of your disagreements. Discuss the issue, not the person. Please refrain from bringing up your partner's flaws to make them feel unsure of themselves or guilt them into agreeing with you.

III. Keep your disagreement about the present and resist the temptation to dredge up old issues and past mistakes.

IV. Stop is combining all your issues and then linking them all into one big problem. Tackle issues as they crop up and find solutions to each. Do not stockpile all your grievances to be used after as some sort of ammunition against your partner.

V. By acknowledging what you may have done wrong, you also encourage others to accept their mistakes. This enables you to resolve and move on from the issue. Stubbornly sticking to your point, even when you know you are wrong, does not do anything to resolve disagreements.

VI. Mind your language. Refrain from using derogatory terms or insults to make a point. Keep the discussion civil and avoid creating animosity. The more you attack the other person, the more closed off they become, and the less likely it is that you will resolve your conflict.

VII. Have a safe space where you can retreat without needing to discuss the conflict. It can be your bedroom or any other place that you feel needs to offer some reprieve from the competition.

VIII. Decide upon a time frame to discuss the issue and bring it to a close. You do not want to keep revisiting the same problem for days on end. Set some time aside and decide that you should both reach a compromise by a lot of that time and let that issue go. It could be an hour, thirty minutes, or as long as you feel you need to address the conflict and resolve it.

Don'ts

I.   Do not try to win by sticking to your point of view, no matter what. If you view conflicts as a battle for supremacy, it will be challenging to get anything resolved.

II. Do not view your partner as your competitor. No matter what, remember you are in the relationship together, and you still need to live with each other once the disagreement has passed.

III. Do not be manipulative. Using threats, aggression, and manipulation to get your way means that the conflict is not resolved. This means sooner or after.

IV. Do not lie. Even when you are afraid of the outcome, resist the urge to be dishonest or mislead your partner. Be open and truthful.

V.   Do not be angry. Getting angry or defensive will get in the way of effective communication if you need to pause the discussion until you are calm enough to engage constructively.

VI. Do not use the past against your partner or to justify your actions. Deal with the current issue without trying to make assumptions based on past experiences.

VII. Do not agree to agree. Express yourself clearly and avoid saying yes only to please the other person. If you make a habit of going along to get along, you will continuously be discontent because you try to suppress your true feelings.

CHAPTER 6:

Increasing Connection with Compassion and Empathy

Uneasiness can torment your connections and can end up being a danger to a couple who have recently begun to understanding and offer the marvels of affection. Regardless of whether you've encountered uneasiness and negative feelings your entire life or have found your weaknesses, it doesn't mean you need to live with them for a fantastic remainder. You can be cheerful and feel love again if you focus on yourself that you'll face, manage them, and get them out of your life.

Practice Self-Assurance

Start with yourself. Be thoughtful to yourself and acknowledge your independence. Grasp what your identity is because these are simply the manners in which you can be guaranteed. A confident individual is sufficiently sure to have confidence in his/her capacities. He better realizes how to lead his/her life and connections. He doesn't search for another person's endorsement. He gets it what it resembles to act naturally.

Self-Compassion

You've presumably practiced sympathy on loved ones. Compassion for others is with a longing to assuage the agony, especially during times of misery. The accentuation is on diminishing suffering. Self-sympathy is simply the demonstration of being merciful, thinking about yourself, deleting your torment, and being with the musings and emotions that are made by your internal pundit without concurring with or utilizing them to hold your story alive.

Probably the ideal approach to develop sympathy for oneself is to locate your inward kid. Envision not being pulled in to hurt and defenseless individual and the desire to comfort him/her and alleviate the torment is practically incomprehensible. They long for some help from the internal pundit's suffering and unhelpful contemplations. Would you be able to envision your internal identity receiving a mindful mentality? Shielding your kid from the inward pundits? When you can get this, you will make a move to be humane towards your "self."

Rehearsing self-sympathy includes relaxing your heart and separating yourself from your internal judgment, and the disdainful comments sustain your dread of dismissal and sentiments of outrage and deficiency. Your internal pundit amplifies each blunder you make. He does so you won't commit similar errors once more. The issue is that the amendments can be extreme to the point that you're left to feel terrible about yourself — so awful that you could make a special effort to forestall only a trace of the "under" you made in any case. It implies you may enjoy maintaining a strategic distance from practices — for instance, if you're apprehensive about disappointment in your connections, you may quit seeking after new propensities or stop facing challenges to keep popping up from the inward pundits.

It would be best if you think the unhelpful propensities in accomplishing your objectives. Be that as it may, your conduct can compound when decisions and negative criticism are connected to the acknowledgment procedure. That is because the excessively negative self-analysis leveled by the inward pundit is hindering; it's identified with discouragement and nervousness. The inward pundit will cause you to feel mindful and protective about your weaknesses, making it more challenging to be straightforward with yourself and assume liability for your demonstrations and mistakes. This can drive you into a diligent condition of accusing others, accusing states, or accusing your story. The work is persuading on the stable association between self-empathy and passionate well-being. Exploration reliably approves that there is a relationship between more prominent self-empathy and less uneasiness and sadness. An essential element of self-sympathy is simply the nonattendance analysis, perceived as a massive marker of tension and wretchedness. Additionally, self-sympathy deactivates the framework identified with sentiments of unreliable connection and protectiveness and triggers oneself soothing system related to feelings of the secure connection and insurance. Self-empathy brings down cortisol levels, which is a pressure hormone. Self-sympathy is additionally an essential part of gainful life in that it is related to sentiments of social connection, enthusiastic knowledge, and life fulfillment.

Make a guarantee, when you were more youthful and give yourself what you would have been given (and might not have been given). It demonstrates that you acknowledge your proceeded with endeavors to do and can be expected instead of rebuffing yourself for not being adequate. Empower yourself to be influenced by your enduring genuinely instead of accusing yourself and along these lines causing all the more torment.

CHAPTER 7:

Healthy Independence

Relationship anxiety is the result of insecurity, which can be toxic to any relationship. If you worry about all kinds of things that can break your relationship, such will loosen the connection between you. When we feel anxious and insecure in our relationships, it may cause us to be clingy and act desperate towards our partner, we become possessive and controlling and attempt to dominate our partner's life, we also tend to punish those we love by being aggressive and taking out our anxiety on them. Therefore, it is essential to deal with relationship anxiety and insecurities before they break our relationships.

Create a Healthy Routine

One way you can deal with relationship anxiety is by starting on a healthy routine. It is hard to make a daily routine and stick to it, but it is possible to be self-disciplined and consistent. Having a healthy way has many benefits. Having a practice helps reduce our stress level.

With a routine, a person feels more in control and less stressed. An exercise helps the uncertainty of things throughout the day as well as improve your sleeping routine. To create a habit, start by doing the following:

Make a List

Write down everything you need to do daily, including both small and big tasks. To ensure a healthy routine add the following functions.

1. **Exercise** — Studies have found that regular exercise can elevate worries, fears, and anxieties in a relationship. On top of relieving relationship anxiety, regular exercise improves sleep, elevates one's mood, increases self-esteem, and boosts self-confidence.

2. **Diet** — The nutritional properties of the foods we eat affect the brain. Studies have shown that brain chemistry can increase or reduce anxiety-related behaviors if essential nutrients are not sufficiently available. Eating healthier ensures that the body and mind receive all the necessary nutrients. On the routine, you also need to set some time apart to shop and cook healthy.

3. **Sleep** — People with relationship anxiety have trouble sleeping, which further adds to their pressure. Getting sufficient sleep recharges, the brain, improves mental well-being, and helps manage any stress or worry that one might be experiencing. Avoid using phones, watching TV, or doing vigorous exercises at least an hour before bedtime. This helps you wind down when it is time to sleep. Sleep no less than 7 hours; it is hard to stick to a routine when you are always tired.

4. **Stay Hydrated** — When you are experiencing the slightest dehydration, you can have a low mood and decreased concentration. Try to reach your recommended water intake by the end of every day.

5. **Relax** — Prolonged anxiety and fear can lead to depression or elevated blood pressure. It is crucial to find an activity that helps you relax. This can be meditating, swimming, going to the spa, or any other relaxing activity.

- **Structure your day** — Depending on what time you work best, divide the above tasks into different parts of your day.
- **Be Specific** — You can get specific and include the time of day each task should be done.
- **Leave room for flexibility** — Sometimes, things do not always go as planned; therefore, it is essential to leave room for flexibility.
- **Test drive the routine** — Start following the pattern, and see how comfortable you are with it. Tweak anything that is not working.

Not following a healthy routine deprives the body and mind of the energy that these activities create. To create a healthy way.

- Start small if you want to eat healthier, change one meal at a time
- Be consistent. Try to do all the activities you have set for yourself by the end of the day.

- Get an accountability partner. When you know you have to explain to someone why you did get your workout in, it pushes you to get it done.
- Track your progress after you finish a task
- When you achieve your weekly goals and are consistent, treat yourself.

Maintaining Your Independence

Successful relationships allow couples to bond together as well as maintain their individuality. Learn to be good together but also right on your own. That way, you can still function optimally when either of you is not present. Avoid relying on your partner for all your needs and wants. People tend to feel insecure when they rely solely on their partners for financial support. Ensure that you have separate friends and experiences from your significant other. Before you started dating, you each had your different friends. It is essential to maintain those friendships. This ensures that your happiness is not dependent only on your partner.

CHAPTER 8:

The wise Relationship

Relationship anxiety is an awful thing to experience. It means you can't enjoy the magic of being in love, so worried you are that your partner's going to fall out of it.

Here Are some easy Ways to Help You Conquer Your insecurity about Relationships.

1. **Know It's All Going to Be Fine.**

   It can quickly feel like the end of the universe when you are amid a falling apart relationship. With all of those emotions running about, putting things in perspective and seeing the light at the end of the tunnel can be incredibly hard. However, you need to know that whatever happens, everything will be perfect. Just think back. You've already had heartbreak before, and you just got through it entirely.

   When you found your partner, you were perfectly acceptable and, difficult as it may be, life would start without them if things were ever going down

Even if your relationship goes down, your life won't stop, and being in a relationship is not your key to heaven. A relationship may be unique, but it never defines who you are

There is nothing you can do about it if someone doesn't want to be with you. If anxiety begins to increase, just whisper to yourself that everything is going to be perfect. When you convince yourself enough, you will continue to believe it sooner or after.

The less you dread the end of the relationship, the more you can settle in and just enjoy it right now.

2. Talk to Your Partner about Your Feelings

A loss of contact or miscommunication is also a cause for insecurity about relationships, and it's essential to be careful and communicate with your partner.

Speak to your partner from a position of authenticity and vulnerability if your partnership is more established, but you still feel uncertain about its future.

Explain how you feel and tell them that your past encounters are not the ones that trigger it. Seek to offer examples of scenarios you find difficult and how they can allay your fears.

If your partner is serious, she will want to do what they can to give you peace of mind.

It can also allow them to communicate their emotions more compassionately when the fear forces you to do something that upsets them. They'll know you don't mean what you're doing all the time, so they can help you conquer your emotions by not adding more fuel to the flames.

The mere act of telling your companion about your anxiety will have you feeling better immediately. You'll feel like a huge weight is off your back, and if they react kindly and lovingly, you'll be more assured they're not going away.

3. Nurture Your Independence.

If you're in love, you might feel like you'd be able to stay in the pocket of your partner if you could, but losing yourself in your relationship is a sure-fire way to increase your anxiety rate.

If you start describing yourself only in terms of your partnership, you are placing too much pressure on the relationship's long-term sustainability. Above all, who would you be if you split? Be sure that you do something for yourself intentionally and have a life apart from your family. Work to retain the qualities that make you unique, which were undoubtedly why your partner was first drawn to you.

Your companion isn't the "other half," so they don't finish you off. You are just as delicate and total as you are.

4. Keep Back from Actively Evaluating Their every Breath.

> People don't think about every word they utter or examine the ways your anxious mind can perceive any text message they send. So, you shouldn't let the smallest things affect your mind.

5. Know You Are the One Controlling Your Mind; It Is Not Your Mind that Is Influencing You.

> You've got the power to steer, shape, and train your mind. You may still experience anxiety until you know it, rather than allow it to overtake you and control your behavior.

6. Avoid Acting on Your Feelings

> Sometimes feeling anxious about your relationship or your partner can make you want proof that everything is OK. Wanting to convince yourself is natural, but avoid the temptation of using this evidence in innocuous or unhelpful ways.

CHAPTER 9:

Maintaining the Fruits of Your Labor

Marriage is a sacred bond developed between you and your spouse, and it is meant to last your entire lifetime. Most people take pride in their marriages because they have found the perfect soul mate who completely understands them.

A marriage can be happy if there are mutual trust and respect; however, this does not mean that things cannot get better for the couple.

Have you considered showering together regularly? It might sound small, but this single action can make your marriage far more exciting. Sharing a shower experience will allow you to develop closer intimacy with your partner and enjoy their presence even in awkward situations.

You do not have to plan to shower together, and the spontaneous suggestion of the two of you jumping under the water together is likely to excite both of you. Taking a shower does not necessarily have to lead to sex, but it will enable both of you to spend some precious time together.

Your partner should be somebody who you enjoy doing light activities with that both of you are interested in. You will be surprised, but simple exercises have the propensity of improving your relationship immensely.

The activities that you do together do not have to be complicated because playing board games, taking nighttime strolls around the neighborhood and even visiting a museum are all activities that can improve the relationship between a couple.

It is always nice to show your partner affection when you are out in public, such as holding hands and kissing him gently on the cheeks. It offers extra commitment on your part and the fact that you are very proud of your partner. Giving your peck of approval in public will go a long way in strengthening your relationship together.

Public affection increases somebody's comfort in a relationship, and it is a sign to the rest of the world that you are together and enjoying your relationship.

Some couples have developed a routine of waking up together very early in the morning to spend quality time together before work. There is no better way of starting the day, such as this, because you can do anything in the early hours, even if it is just talking in bed before setting off to work.

You will be surprised how comfortable your day will be, although it might subject you to be sleeping early when you return home.

Be very encouraging with your spouse, whether in their professional life or handling something difficult in their lives. Showing encouragement is a sign of positivity, and this will endear your partner to you in an incredible way.

When you continually support their work, they feel a closer connection to you like no other person. There is no more incredible feeling than knowing you have somebody in your corner who is ready to encourage you even through the thickest of problems.

You will be surprised that a relationship on the brink of collapse can be improved immensely merely by the couple telling each other of their love. It is a very comfortable feeling, and it confirms that there is nobody else significant in your partner's life other than yourself.

It is possible to make healthy memories with him even though you have endured tough times in your relationship by setting aside time to talk to each other. This can be an excellent time to solve pertinent problems affecting the two of you so that you can move the relationship forward.

A relationship will always improve tremendously if both of you understand the value of each other's time. It is essential to respect their interests as much as they will yours, and this interaction together will always improve a relationship even if it has endured several difficulties along the way.

These useful strategies can be implemented in most marriages to help them overcome common problems affecting couples. The advice should prompt you to take action and never sit around complaining about your spouse when you can take action yourself.

It is necessary to point out that action is always needed to improve any relationship as long as there is love between them.

CHAPTER 10:

Tips for Non-Anxious Partners

The spouse or non-anxious partner of an anxious person recognizes that their role in the process is as a supporter.

Tip 1: Understand that Overcoming Anxiety Is a Process (Anxiety Is Not Something that Someone Will Snap Out of)

Anxiety is not like having a common cold. It is not something that you get, and you will experience resolution from a finger's snap. Anxiety disorders should be thought of as conditions that require treatment. This defines that you should be realistic about your partner's anxiety for the significant other of an anxious person. As a supporter of an anxious person, it is critical to recognize that you will be helping them through the long process of overcoming their illness.

Tip 2: Be conscious of Your Dysfunctional Thoughts or Preconceived Notions

Anxiousness is characterized by a cavalcade of dysfunctional thoughts that people often are not conscious of. Unfortunately, for the significant others of anxious persons, they can spiral dysfunctional ideas that can impact how they perceive and interact with their anxious partner. The meaning here is not that the partner is necessarily at risk for worry, but merely that the partner should recognize how notions can color their interaction with their partner that they have about their condition (including the subconscious stigma that men and women often have towards needs of the mind).

Tip 3: Provide Reassurance that Things Are Going to Turn Out all right

One of the most important things that someone is supporting someone else through anxiety (or any condition) can reassure that things will turn out all right. This does not mean telling a lie. If someone has a terminal illness like stage IV cancer, it is essential to recognize precisely what that means. But honest reassurance in the case of anxiousness is a little different. Anxiety can and does frequently get better, so reminding your partner of that can place a positive thought in their head that can be an essential part of creating real change in their life.

Tip 4: Encourage Your Partner to Get Help

A complicated reality for some partners of anxious people to accept is that it is not their job to steer their partner in the direction they think they should go.

Intervention-type maneuvers can be problematic in mental health. Forcing or cornering your partner into treatment is not a good idea for anxious people. You can educate yourself about the help that is available for their condition and encourage them to get help. That is all that you can do.

Tip 5: Be patient as Your Significant Other Moves through Their Condition

Recall that anxiety disorders include conditions as divergent as GAD, specific phobias, and obsessive-compulsive disorder. For your sanity (and for your partner), it is essential to be patient. The change will happen slowly, and it will help you to keep this in mind.

Tip 6: Provide ongoing Education and Support to Your Partner

You are being supportive means being someone that your significant other can go to when they need help. Again, the goal here is not to force your partner to do something that they may not be ready to do but to support them as they decide to change and take steps towards making that change. As a supportive partner, you can provide ongoing education for yourself about anxiety and related conditions like depression. You can even find ways to pass this information along to your partner.

Tip 7: Recognize that no one Understands Your Partner's Anxiety more than Your Partner

You may be around them for several hours of the day. You may feel that you may see aspects of their concern that they may seem unconscious of, but as you are not experiencing what they are and are not inside their head to know what the triggers are, you perhaps do not understand their condition as well as you might think.

Tip 8: Be available, Not overbearing

You may find that you have an overweening desire to help them, and perhaps you feel that you can see matters from a vantage point that they may not see. Even if that is the case, your partner does have the ability and the right to make decisions for themselves. Loved one or not, you do not necessarily have the right to force them to do as you want them to do if they are not a danger to themselves or others.

Tip 9: Take Your Partner's Comments Seriously

You learn the character of your partner's anxiousness (and gain a deep sense of what they are going through) by talking to them.

Your partner's anxiety is just that, their anxiety, and you need to leave it to them to clue you in on how they are feeling and why. Therefore, it is vital as a supportive partner to talk to your partner and to exercise active listening. Just as your anxious partner may hang on to your every word, you need to learn to pay attention to your partner's terms. When your partner tells you something about themselves or what they are going through, take it seriously.

Tip 10: Remember that Empathy Is important

Sympathy is a word that many people understand, although they do not always show it. Empathy involves feeling compassion and tolerance for others, which comes from a deep understanding of where the other person is coming from.

We can show sympathy for others through our words, our actions, or even by our facial expressions. But empathy is something different. Empathy involves sharing the feelings of others: experiencing what they are experiencing.

Conclusion

nxiety does not have to derail your life or the life of your spouse. Suppose you are in a relationship where anxiety is a matter of concern. In that case, you can take comfort in understanding that anxiety symptoms can be successfully handled in several ways, easing the grip that anxious thoughts have on your relationship. One of this tome's purposes has been to show the reader what they're thinking to understand. Part of what makes anxiety so challenging to handle in relationships is that many people do not understand what anxiety makes a simple act of acknowledgment difficult.

I have a picture in my mind of you now. You are sitting under an umbrella on the beach, an ice-cold margarita in the sand beside you. Your hair is down, and you're wearing sunglasses. As I walk past you, I can't help but notice your smile. Even though I can see you're sleeping, your smile is naturally painted on your face. Your smile makes me chuckle, in the right way, of course. But there's one thing that stands out to me. You are lying beside your partner, and even though both of you are sleeping, you're holding hands, and both have that natural smile on your face. I picture your relationship as one that is envied.

This is what I wish for you. I hope that you've created the kind of relationship that other people wish they had. People will walk by you every day and say: "Wow, I want to be like them. They're the picture of a healthy relationship, and they will grow old together." This has been a long journey for the two of you, and you deserve nothing less than happiness. Now that the two of you have completed your journey, and you have recreated yourselves and your relationship, my work is done. Never stop smiling and never forget the way you both feel at this exact moment in time.

Uneasiness influences the individual who has it and every individual who manages it – and in a relationship, its outcomes might be considerably more adverse and significant, regardless of how steady the accomplice may be.

I hope to see the single men and women who read this find the right person. Remember never to stop looking. There is a lid for every pot out there, and if you give up, you will miss out.

To those of you who have been through hell and back and used this guide to re-enter the game of companionship, I salute you. Make me proud; more importantly, make yourselves proud.

And lastly, to the person who stood by their partner through thick and thin, I just want to say: You made it!

Whoever you are, take a massive sigh of relief now. The hard part is over, and you're finally able to breathe. Remember to maintain your relationship because you know how hard it was to get here.

Now go out there and be the poster child for a healthy, long-lasting, anxiety-free relationship.

Part Two:

Couples Therapy Workbook

CHAPTER 1:

What Is Couples Therapy?

Couples therapy (also referred to as marital therapy, marriage counseling, pair counseling, etc.) is a specialized form of family therapy where intimate partners are the object of intervention or therapy. Family therapy is a specific form of group therapy where more than one associated individual is treated simultaneously (in the same session). Counseling for couples has been beneficial. This leads to better relationships, problem solutions, or fewer feelings of distress. But if therapy is so useful, why do people often hesitate to start again?

Fortunately, the counseling process has excellent benefits that you will lose if your anxiety doesn't stop you. On the one hand, you don't do it alone. The couple's therapist is a neutral party who is not interested in the outcome as friends and family do. Also, therapy will provide you with tools that, as a couple, will allow you to share your thoughts and feelings effectively. Couple therapy teaches you how to listen and talk about difficult issues with your spouse. You will learn to stay connected when you hear something that overwhelms your body with strong emotions. Effective marriage counseling teaches you how to speak for yourself and negotiate your needs and wants while empowering your partner. It provides a forum for you to practice putting yourself in the shoes of your partner, which is incredibly difficult when you disagree. Many skills will be learned and practiced under the supervision of a couple's therapist, and the result is likely to be personal growth and increased intimacy.

Whether you are dealing with infidelity, daily duels, or the threat of a romantic relationship, your marriage may already be deeply disturbed, and what it looked like is not a viable strategy. Ignoring your problems and hoping for improvement can be a risky decision. So even if the counseling process sometimes hurts, it's worth it. While it's important to point out that if there is a very qualified therapist, no specific treatment or outcome can be guaranteed, you can face your fears or lose everything you have.

Seeking help from a team of counselors is a proactive decision. The marriage counselor is the third pair of eyes and ears when it comes to couples in need.

When couples undergo therapy together to resolve their differences and restore their love and trust, the goals and limits must be established. One of the goals of couple therapy is to create or improve lines of communication. Most of the time, the root of marital conflicts lies in the lack of proper communication between societies. This is also why specific needs are not met, and misunderstandings occur between couples.

Another objective of counseling couples is to regain a sense of commitment lost during the marriage. Marriage is a joy, but it can also be overwhelmed by events that can trigger a couple's engagement. Counselors can help couples develop the commitment they initially had by rethinking the issues that caused the meeting's termination. Couples can create other modes of communication and understanding to resolve. For couples, the challenge is to go beyond a sensitive subject. However, with a counselor who can pave the way for learning and healing, you can certainly help couples grow more robust and prosper as wiser beings.

Through counseling, married couples will learn to understand that their relationship with their children can also be compromised when marital problems invade the home. They can begin to solve their problems and move forward with a positive outlook on their relationship as married couples and household heads. When couples decide to fight for a healthy relationship, everyone involved also receives benefits. Also, couple counseling aims to improve the couple as an individual and as a married couple. Through counseling, people learn a lot about themselves. They are aware that all their actions affect the partner, and sensitivity and understanding play an essential role in maintaining a happy and happy married life — the life they want to build together.

The most important Question Is How It Works?

Thus, couple therapy involves specific generic tasks such as matching in various activities, or particular tasks such as writing the partner's best and worst properties to redefine a relationship.

The therapy begins with a conventional interview of the married couple about themselves, their family, values, and morals. The conversations are recorded or recorded by the advisor.

Then, the problem areas were identified, and the treatment orientation was established. The couple is then asked to speak to confirm their emotional distress and level of interaction. Each dysfunctional communication is noticed. The therapist can even examine close friends or family to find out more about the situation. Then a detailed analysis is carried out based on all the observations.

Sometimes most of the problems are due to poor communication, and the therapist establishes a solid ground for communicating with couples. Reports and issues are resolved so that both are understood. Tasks such as cooking together or painting or similar activities are given to understand each other better. Often, many marriages are saved by simple couple therapy.

No need to break your heart and give up when you can seek help from a professional. Find the right therapist in your field, do your research, and try this therapy.

CHAPTER 2:

How to Recognize Toxic and Unhealthy Behavior?

A nxiety isn't always the element that affects a relationship. Sometimes it's the other path around, and the reason you have anxiety is because of a toxic relationship. But what exactly does toxic mean? We refer to a toxic relationship when it isn't beneficial to you, and it's harmful somehow. The building blocks for a healthy relationship are made from mutual respect and admiration, but sometimes it just isn't enough. However, there is a difference between a problematic relationship and a toxic one, mainly the noxious atmosphere surrounding you. This kind of relationship can suffocate you with time and prevent you from living a happy, productive life. Many factors lead to toxicity. It is most often caused by friction between two people who are opposites of each other. In others, nothing specific is to blame, and the toxic relationship grows from the lack of communication, the establishment of boundaries, and the ability to agree on something, or at the very least, compromise.

Take note that not all toxic relationships develop because of the couple. Sometimes there is an outlier seeking to influence conflict because they will benefit from it in some way. This type of individual preys on other people's insecurities, weaknesses, or manipulates his way inside a relationship from which he has something to gain. In some cases, a toxic person seeks to destroy a relationship to get closer to one of them.

Personal needs, emotions, and goals take priority over anyone else's well-being.

With that in Mind, Let's Briefly Explore the Characteristics of a Toxic Relationship:

1. Poisonous: A relationship that is extremely unpleasant to be around as it poisons the atmosphere around it. It makes anyone around the couple anxious, and it can even lead to psychological and emotional problems such as anxiety and depression.

2. Deadly: Toxic relationships are bad for your health.

    In many cases, it involved risky, destructive, and abusive behaviors. Some people end up harming themselves with alcohol, drugs, or worse. Injuries and even death can become the final result.

3. Negative: In this kind of relationship, negativity is the norm. There is no positive reinforcement, even when children are involved. The overwhelming lack of approval and emotional support is standard.

4. Harmful: Toxic relationships, lack balance, and awareness. Those involved are never truly aware of each other and lack the most positive principles that a healthy relationship needs. Toxicity also promotes immoral and malicious acts that harm a romantic relationship.

As mentioned earlier, toxic relationships don't always involve psychopaths or those who display similar traits. In many situations, these relationships are the way they are due to decent people who are terrible decision-makers or lack social skills. Taking a wrong turn in life happens to everyone, and many people change, but not always for the better.

Warning Signs

Now that you can better identify toxic relationships and the kind of involved people, let's see if you're in one or not. Humans are complex creatures, and the traits don't necessarily make someone toxic. Some underlying issues and disorders can make people behave negatively. However, they can still be excellent partners.

With that said, here's a list of questions you can ask yourself to learn more about your relationship:

1. How do you feel in the company of your partner?

2. Do you feel happy, safe, and nurtured in the presence of your significant other?

3. Are all the other people involved in your relationship safe and happy? For instance, your

children (if you have any), parents, friends, and so on. As mentioned earlier, people tend to avoid toxic relationships instead of being in contact with them.

4.   Do you experience anxiety or panic attacks when discussing something with your partner?

5.   Can you think of any scenarios in which you were manipulated to do something that wasn't for your best interest?

6.   Is your partner pushing the limits of what you would consider ethical? Is he or she even crossing the line of what is legal?

7.   Does your partner to push you to perform challenging tasks that you consider entirely unnecessary? These challenges may seem pointless, and that you need to resolve just because it's what your partner wants.

8.   Do you feel emotionally strained and exhausted after interacting with your partner?

Handling a toxic Relationship

As mentioned, a toxic relationship can be a powerful source of anxiety. It doesn't have to be a romantic relationship either. Some of them you can avoid by cutting contact with some people to feel relief. However, there are certain people you simply cannot break away from, whether they are romantic partners or your mother in law.

The first step is to accept the inescapable situation. When your options are limited, you cannot achieve relief by avoidance, and acceptance leads to a decrease in anxiety. You may be tempted to be hostile towards that person, but it won't help. Instead, it will just add to your worries and stress. At this point, your only alternative is managing your anxiety by admitting to yourself that you may never be able to get along with that person. Besides, you can attempt to ignore him or her entirely by never spending time together and ignoring any contact. However, none of these tactics usually work.

Accept that this relationship is complicated and challenges you, but you do your best to make it better. That doesn't mean you should completely surrender. Accepting your situation will allow yourself new possibilities and new options instead of repeatedly punishing yourself.

Take note that you need to be consciously aware that you are not responsible for anyone else's emotions and reactions for the process of acceptance to take hold. Toxic behavior often makes people blame you for their situation and feelings. Do not accept any of that, as you are not the reason for their suffering. They need to take responsibility for their thoughts and actions instead of blaming others.

The second step is telling the truth. If a toxic relationship is creating stress, you often lie to avoid conflict, causing even more anxiety. The problem is that when you lie to such a person, you enable them and become partially responsible for the reality they create — leading to the toxic environment surrounding them.

CHAPTER 3:

How Can You Benefit from
Couples Therapy?

When someone struggles with their mental health, therapy can be beneficial regardless of whether they have a diagnosed condition. The same goes for relationships, whether there is a significant problem or not. Many people believe couples counseling is just for people on the verge of a breakdown, but the reality is that just about every couple can benefit. Communication can be very tricky, and there are ups and downs in every relationship.

A good counselor can facilitate difficult conversations, provide insight into what couples are trying to say, or help a couple with communication techniques.

Reasons to Consider Couples Therapy

When should a couple consider therapy? There are many scenarios where a relationship can benefit from a third party's advice and guidance, and they aren't all emotionally catastrophic.

Here are seven:

You Don't Trust each other

Either through emotional or physical cheating, lying about money, or lies about anything, the relationship stalls or starts to break down if there is no trust. Either one person within the couple or both no longer feel safe and secure. A therapist can help heal the division, facilitate vulnerability, and offer guidance on what to do after.

You Fight all the Time

Fighting with your partner more than you usually do, it's a sign that something is wrong. It could be about anything small or big. The issue is that most of your communication becomes contentious and stressful.

You Don't Communicate well

You don't have to conflict with your partner to benefit from therapy. Sometimes, you and your partner don't "get" each other. Communication-wise, it feels like you are ships passing in the night. It's always a struggle to express your thoughts and feelings about things, and you frequently feel misunderstood or even ignored. On the other hand, you might feel disconnected from your partner and unable to get anything out of them emotionally. Maybe both are present in your relationship. A therapist can help you safely break down walls, be more vulnerable, and learn to communicate more.

You're Going Through a huge Life Change

Change is always tricky for a relationship, even if it's good to change. It can throw off your regular routines, emotional state, and even your identity. Changes in relationships can include moving house, getting a new job, losing a job, losing a loved one, having kids, and soon. They can help you and your partner be vulnerable and honest with each other, understand each other more, and strengthen your bond.

Physical Intimacy Is a Point of Conflict

Everyone (and every couple) is different when it comes to physical intimacy. It can cause many conflicts, especially if one person in the relationship feels rejected, neglected, or pressured physically. It's a sensitive and emotional topic, and frustrations can flare. A therapist can help keep things cool and collected and provide a safe space for vulnerability and honesty.

Mental Health Issues

Navigating a relationship can be especially tricky if only one person has the diagnosis and has trouble communicating their needs to their partner. Maybe you have social anxiety and wish your partner would be more considerate about triggers, or your partner (who isn't mentally ill) is confused about what to do when you go through a depression episode. A therapist can help you two communicate and understand each other better.

Something Feels "Off"

Therapy isn't just for couples who know exactly what they want to talk about. If something feels "off" or wrong about your relationship, you should strongly consider therapy. A therapist can help you identify areas and triggers where the discomfort is most potent, and express your feelings and fears to your partner in an exact, honest way. It may turn out that you two just needed a third party to help clarify some things, or it may reveal more profound issues that you can focus on.

What Couples Therapy Isn't

Couples therapy is not a magic solution to all of your problems as a couple or individual. Couples therapy should teach you better communication, but communicating better may reveal things that let you know the relationship shouldn't continue. This isn't easy to hear, but it's essential to accept that going to couple's therapy may not give you the happy ending you expect.

Couples therapy should also not be treated as something that only happens in the therapist's office. Don't plan on going once a week or once every two weeks and not doing anything else. That won't improve communication between you and your partner. Like regular therapy, most of the work is done outside of that hour or so window. The therapist's job is to help identify conflict areas, advise on what to do, and facilitate dialogue.

CHAPTER 4:

Attachment Theory Basics

Knowing both the attachment styles of yourself and your partner can be of incomparable benefit to your relationship. Being able to anticipate both parties' behavior within a relationship – and the possible obstacles you will face can help smooth the path to a healthier, long-lasting connection.

Let's Take a Glance at what to Get When People with each Attachment Type Form a Couple:

Secure + secure

While secure couples in relationships have problems just like everybody else, their relationship is often characterized by excellent communication and empathy. They resolve conflicts more easily and know that they can rely on each other, in good times and bad.

The secure + secure coupling is the most common type of relationship, owing to many people in the population with secure attachment styles, and secures' abilities to cultivate healthy, long-lasting relationships.

Anxious preoccupied + secure

In this relationship combination, the anxious preoccupied partner is likely to test the secure partner's patience by seeking regular assurance. If the secure partner does not act quickly, the edgy, obsessed partner can become anxious and stressed. Despite their inherent securities, this behavior can test the secure partner's patience and cause them to act distantly or pull away, much as a dismissive-avoidant would.

However, a secure partner can be of great benefit to an anxious preoccupied person. The safe can cultivate their partner's trust in the relationship through patient and constant reassurance.

In such a combination, the secure partner can often feel as though they are responsible for the relationship's upkeep and security. The anxious preoccupied insecurities can become self-centered, causing the secure partner to think that their loved one is not invested in the relationship.

Through gentle reassurance from the secure partner, however, this problem should improve over time.

Dismissive avoidant + secure

When partnered with a dismissive-avoidant, a person will often experience distance and coldness within a relationship. This behavior can cause even the most secure people to feel attachment anxiety, leading them to question their self-worth. Even though the securer's requests for assurance will likely be reasonable, the dismissive-avoidant partner will usually not respond to these requests.

For such a combination to work, the secure partner must be aware of their partner's issues and demonstrate enormous amounts of patience to cultivate more security and openness with the relationship.

They are comfortable and confident enough to know someone out there will treat them right in their abilities and self-worth.

Fearful avoidant + secure

This combination has much in common with the dismissive-avoidant + secure pairing. However, the difference is that it is likely to be the fearful-avoidant partner who ends the relationship at the first sign of trouble. This behavior comes about thanks to the fearful, avoiding's fear of being seen for who they are. They are afraid of loss and believe that ending the relationship on their terms will be far less painful than their partner's rejection. They often come to think that this rejection is inevitable, once the fast breaks through the fearful avoiding's façade.

Dismissive avoidant + anxious preoccupied

This potentially damaging combination is one of the most common. The anxious preoccupied will seek the dismissive-avoidant inconsistent attention because of an unconscious need to replay their childhood events. The dismissive-avoidant undervalues their partner, while the anxious distracted overvalues them, leading to a relationship characterized by stress and anxiety.

While the dismissive-avoidant likes to shy away from intimacy and connection, their needy partner will act to confirm the dismissive avoiding's view that all people are clingy. This confirmation makes the dismissive-avoidant more comfortable in the relationship than they would otherwise be, and they often settle into this coupling for the long-haul.

Fearful avoidant + anxious preoccupied

This coupling is among the most negative and damaging. It is also one of the most insecure collars. The anxious preoccupied partner's constant need for attention will scare off the fearful-avoidant partner, who will usually be unwilling to be involved in a relationship in which they are continually fending off intimacy. If the fearful-avoidant partner acquiesces to their partner's need for closeness, it will likely trigger their anxiety. Conversely, if they remain in their comfort zone and keep their distance, the anxious preoccupied partner will respond by increasing their requests for attention.

Anxious preoccupied + anxious preoccupied

This is another coupling that very rarely has a happy ending. The often self-absorbed anxious preoccupied will have trouble anticipating the needs and desires of their partner. With both partners having a deep-seated need for attention and closeness, it is unlikely — although not impossible Do's that they will be able to satisfy each other's desires.

Fearful avoidant + dismissive avoidant

This partnership is an uncommon one, due to both parties being wrong at the positive attachment. Even though both partners may want a less "hands-on" approach to the relationship on the surface, the fearful-avoidant has a deep-seated need for affection that the dismissive-avoidant will rarely fill.

Dismissive avoidant + dismissive avoidant

Unsurprisingly, this coupling is very rare. Cultivating a relationship requires communication — something dismissive-avoidant seek to avoid — a relationship between two people with this attachment style rarely gets off the ground. If they manage to form a relationship, they are prone to ending it at the first hint of conflict, to avoid communicating and resolving it.

Fearful avoidant + fearful avoidant

This is the most uncommon matching, but this is primarily because there is only a small number of fearful avoidant people in the general population. The fearful avoiding's difficulties with communication and self-esteem will make this coupling a challenge. However, it is not necessarily doomed to fail. As both parties have a deep-seated need for intimacy, there is the chance that they can satisfy this need for each other.

CHAPTER 5:

Negative Relationships Cycles

Modern wedding vows have an exquisite symmetry: for evil, or worse. Yet love isn't perfectly straight, and many people don't know it could be skewed. The worst in marriage, or some other relation, means so much more than that best. This is what the brain functions.

Imagine meeting someone that does something which makes you irritated. (This does not take much imagination). Maybe your partner's a big spender, or fascinated with your mates, or spaced out in the center of your narratives. How would you react?

1. Just let slip, and pray things to get better.

2. Discuss what's troubling you and seeking a solution.

3. Sulk. Speak nothing and emotionally detach from your mate.

4. Move over to the exit. It is challenging to split up or consider searching for a new mate.

Those responses build a matrix about how dating partners address issues. Psychologists defined two basic, destructive or constructive methods, both of which may be either active or passive. The pragmatic solutions seemed responsive and noble but little counted. Staying passively faithful has a little discernible effect on the couple's relationships course; attempting to figure out a compromise consciously only changed things a little.

How negative Attitude Turns Up in Relationships?

Differentiating pathological sadness from positive manifestations of unhappy or depressed feelings and real emotional problems, such as anxiety or depression, is essential.

Obviously, during difficult moments, or when somebody is emotionally unwell, stress can worsen. But a severely pessimistic individual will regularly display six or seven of the symptoms underneath:

- Accept incredibly sensitive little slights or feedback from a mate.

- Still assume the worse in daily life and probably in the partnership.

- Good events/interactions flow out and reflect on the bad.

- Choose claims over specific matters.

- Sometimes moody or irritable with relatives or girlfriend.

- Most highly-critical spouses are always the highest of the rankings.

- Welcome the proposals of friends with a justification they won't fit or tell 'no' to recommendations before they can think 'please.'

- Everything to overthink. (For example, fixating; over-taking of experiences or encounters).

- Competing for sincere appreciation or encouragement.

- Want to think you don't want people.

- Fail to take comfort in ordinary things.

- Punishing others for everything like friends.

- Problems are coping with rejection, dismissal, or negative news.

- Has trouble viewing oneself in the right way.

How to Flip Things Around?

Chronic depression also has deep, gnarly origins to trace it back to your upbringing or personal past. You can't help, but it's worth attempting to change things around, which can significantly impact future life and family. Here's how:

Shut Your Mouth

It doesn't sound analytical, but many, maybe most, of our answers are automatic or conditioned, particularly with individuals we're familiar with. Whoosh, they're out of the lips before we thoroughly understand what we're doing, and that's especially valid when criticism has become a routine. A therapist can remind you that in a pause, there's a tremendous strength. Every day, we use it for ourselves. So, pause just until you say something. And, perhaps, there is simply no need at all to speak?

Examine the Reality and Legitimacy of Thinking

Let's imagine you just informed your spouse she'll look awful for the latest photo she needs to put on a specific wall. Check your ideas. Is this real, then? Can you know for sure? And if it seems terrible, isn't she able to figure something out by herself? And if, because you don't, she likes it, then can't it stay on the window ledge? Do interior decor's exclusive rights remain to you?

Recall that the firm views aren't inherently truth-based. And sometimes though they are, indeed, they're your reality that may be unique from your spouse's. But aim to see theirs.

Don't Focus to Just Be "positive"

That's like asking somebody who is starting to quit cheesecake entirely. It is so intense, and the desire for cheesecake just turns up. Instead, seek also to be neutralized. When anyone makes you don't want an idea, push yourself to remain responsive to the chance. Assert yourself that you are an "open-minded individual" and claim to others as well: this is an admirable trait (as much as you intend that). A more assertive approach than pretending to remain constructive is to show a smile or a compliment. It can look at first sound unfamiliar, but it lasts. If it is real, so you can build respect with your spouse as well as yourself.

Avoid Complaining

Concerning your job, your manager, your well-being, your problems, the temperature, and the things that pushed your garbage bin. We just need to talk, and ideally, your spouse will be able to respond to your sincere issues. But — above this — no-one deserves to listen any of the mind's derogatory stuff. It's reasonable enough to have those ideas, however-okay-get a newspaper — a puppy. If you're nice to your puppy, they'll enjoy you beyond question.

A negative Mindset Isn't About Making You Seem wise

Critical thinkers also hang on to the illusion. After all, their negative answers make them appear wise because they have been trained to see cleverly when something might go wrong.

Currently, the reverse is occurring. An individual who reacts negatively habitually is sometimes seen as logically static or even constrained, instead of smart. It might seem like you don't look at things from every perspective, or can't. You just have one set vision-your own. In every relation, that will offer you less control. Want to be treated this way?

Sit-in for the Fear

Negativity is most often motivated by anxiety dwelling over what ended up going wrong last time or thinking about what might go astray in the long term. We always assume that when we feel nervous, we would either (a) convey that or (b) take some action. But it's suitable only to accept it and live with it-if we offer them time and room, evil thoughts and emotions slip away.

CHAPTER 6:

Typical Relationship Problems and How to Solve Them

Are We Both Willing to Change our Habits?

There is one pervasive problem that comes from resolving our frustrations with our spouse's habits. When someone denies that the habit is wrong, it leaves their partner feeling frustrated while simultaneously cutting off any resolution possibility.

In dialectic behavior therapy, we must consider our spouse's frustrations as valid if we want to have any hope of resolving the problem. It is another issue of whether you want to be right or loved.

You may believe your habit is acceptable, and even if you completely do not understand why your partner would think otherwise, you need to accept the fact that they are truly upset about it. Your spouse is not "wrong" for feeling the way they do.

Recall our lesson about the importance of subjectivity in communication in a relationship. Everyone thinks they are right. This is a very human thing. We believe that our partner is crazy for not agreeing with us, in the same way, we think that all the people who do not share all our views on significant issues must be crazy.

You must keep in mind that other people do not all think the same way; they all think they are just as right as you do. Any time you are trying to act like you are better than your spouse for not having the habits they have, try to keep in mind that you do things that bother them.

It is not the habits themselves that are the core issue, although you can both work on those habits. The core issue is learning how to be more tolerant of what your spouse does, even if it annoys you.

How to Strengthen our Relationship?

Besides the last question, this second-to-last one depends on the most on the quality of communication you had with your spouse for every other problem. You cannot make yourself a better, healthier couple before confronting all the broader issues we addressed.

You are armed with the emotional understanding you have now. It is up to the two of you to figure out how you will work together. How will you ensure the problems you had the last time you tried to make up will not come up again?

The answer to the first question at least has something you can fall back on. If the two of you find that the same problems come up again — even ones that you thought, you worked through in here — you should read back through it and see what insights you can find here.

As much as I believe in the insights written below the dialectical behavior therapy questions, I am referring to the insights you get from each other during your discussions.

What is more important than anything you read in these pages is what you say to each other in your conversations. Even the conversation topics can go by the wayside if you learn how to have productive, open discussions.

Any relationship problem can be resolved if both people in the couple know how to have this kind of conversation. It is a conversation where both can say whatever they want without having to be afraid.

Where Are We Headed as a Couple? Where Will We Be in 5 Years?

This question is highly intertwined with the one when you see your spouse as a crucial part of your life. Think past yourself and think about you, your spouse, and your household.

For the last question, I asked you to hold off on thinking about the two of you as a unit for the question's extent. I wanted you to think only about yourself and where you might end up.

Do not see this question as totally separate from the last one. Instead, ask yourself how the future you imagined for yourself as an individual fit into this future with your spouse and family.

Simultaneously, do not let the enormous life shift that a divorce would become the thing that prevents you from getting it. If a divorce is what you as a couple need, then you should agree and go through with it.

But it is not likely that this is the case since you are nearly at the end of our relationship. If you did not have any hope that your relationship could get better, then you would not have come this far. So, you should take this opportunity to figure out what kind of future the two of you imagine for each other.

What Now?

The final question is no longer about what you will do to work together in general. You must both face your vices and strengths and make up your mind on what you will do now in this specific situation.

At first, you do not want to go back to the questions you already answered, unless they call to you. When you reach this last question, your mind should already be formulating something about what you will do.

When you come to one decision together, bring everything you have learned into it, remembering the mistakes you made before, so you do not make them again. They say maintaining a healthy marriage is a 24/7 job, and it is not just a cliché.

CHAPTER 7:

Best Relationship-Strengthening Activities for Couples

When you decide to strengthen a relationship, try to give your best to improve the connection. If you have already found the individual with whom you would like to spend the rest of your life and want to start the relationship on the right foot, there are specific points that you will need to remember:

- Have common values and visions: If one of you keeps spending all the time while the other keeps saving money, if one of you keeps maintaining a proper diet while the other keeps having junk foods, if one of you is on one side of the political spectrum while the other is on either side, etc., the chances are high that fights will keep taking place. Such differences will lead to frequent conflicts. For lasting the relationship, you will need to prepare a set of commonalities for which both of you can come together. Try to have a shared vision that will help you and your partner project the relationship into a shining future. Doing this will help in sharing dreams and will also establish a good understanding between partners.

- Please each other and try to give recognition: The most common thing that tends to destroy most relationships is when partners take each other for granted. When you stop yourself from putting in efforts into the relationship, you take the relationship for granted. For example, when you do not nurture your relationship when you keep criticizing now and then when you ignore your partner's struggles and believe that your partner will love you without even doing anything for the relationship. It is not the way how relationships work out. Both partners need to recognize each other for both partners in a healthy relationship to feel appreciated and loved. You are required to show gratitude to your partner and vice versa. This type of attitude can nurture collaboration, encourage a steady connection, and help the partners appreciate each other. No matter what happens in the relationship, never take your partner and the relationship for granted.

- Be proud of your partner: Is it possible to live happily in a relationship if you cannot even admire your partner? The answer is no. There is no need for your romantic partner to win a Nobel Prize or a trophy for being praised by the person whom they love, which you are. If you cannot even appreciate at least a single trait of your partner, no matter if it is beauty, intelligence, courage, determination, or humor, you do not appreciate your partner's existence in your life. Human beings tend to gravitate towards all those who express acceptance, love, and fulfillment towards them. Give your best efforts to make your romantic partner feel accepted and loved all the time. Just appreciate him/her in the relationship, and you will be able to maintain the spark in your relationship.

- Try having realistic expectations: Some women are always searching for an impossible Prince Charming. They tend to believe that romantic relationships will always look like a fairy tale. Talking about men, they might get influenced by the standards that are being set by the media. No matter what sort of unfounded expectations you keep inside yourself, if they tend to be unrealistic, they are most likely to generate disappointment in your relationship. It is always better to have modest and realistic expectations regarding your relationship. Always remember, a relationship is not an easy game. You will need to fight various obstacles to giving it a proper shape. Instead of just setting up unrealistic expectations, try to shift your focus on the betterment of the relationship.

- Provide affection daily: It has been found that long-lasting relationships are the ones in which the partners have been capable of replacing passion and love gradually with attachment. Affection, tenderness, and cuddling help in oxytocin production, which is the hormone responsible for attachment. If you are willing to feed in your partner's well-being, never forget to show the power of affection.

- Do not allow the sexual flame to blow out: The initial phases of a relationship are always filled with passion and affection. With passing time, the frequency of making love to your partner gets reduced gradually. All of this can be the result of various reasons, for which you cannot blame each other. If this continues, sexual desire will slowly get extinguished. You will find it tough to reignite the spark, no matter how much you try. Sexual desire plays a vital role in the well-being of a relationship. The real key to this problem is to give enough time for intimacy in the relationship. Regardless of how busy you are throughout the day, keep showing small gestures that can help keep the spark alive. For example, text your partner to be ready before you reach home, plan a romantic candlelight dinner, text your partner that you love them, appreciate your partner's body, and many others. It all depends on the small gestures that can make a relationship successful.

- Exercise daily, eat well, and stay healthy for keeping the flame ignited despite the passing time. The taste of the partners is another thing that also comes into play. It can easily fit into a more generalized vision that can also benefit your health and personal development.

- Being open about improving yourself: If both partners keep living in a constant state of self-denial and pride, the relationship is preparing for doom. Being in a healthy relationship means improving yourself every day, opting for compromises, understanding the mistakes and shortcomings, and giving your best for correcting them. People who have the habit of being proud of themselves all the time generally avoid this subject intentionally. They try to move their focus from all the faults and mistakes. If you have such a habit, your partner will find it challenging to be in a relationship. You will need to learn to improve yourself daily. As you keep being proud of yourself, you will gradually shift your partner's attention towards you.

- Staying faithful: Being faithful indicates going out of the boundary of egotism. Being egoistic will make you prioritize your pleasures while keeping aside the needs and interests of your partner. If you think that you genuinely love a person, deceiving that person will be the last thought on your mind. Love is the most decadent experience of our lives that needs to be lived with hardships and happiness. Why undermine the value of love with unfaithfulness and lies? In simple terms, romantic relationships are dynamic, just like life. For enriching such relationships, you will need first to acknowledge that your point of view is not the ultimate point of view.

Strong connections are bound to form when you learn to accept your responsibility to make an effort and understand your partner's perspective.

CHAPTER 8:

Worksheets and Technique for Couples

Tips to Make a strong Connection in Your Relationship:

1. Accept the Uniqueness of Your Partner

We have all had times wishing our partner were leaner, more prosperous, and more romantic, etc. Look at your goals and ask how achievable they are. According to my research, unrealistic expectations contribute to constant disappointment, which is the crucial reason why relationships collapse.

2. For Communicating, Take 10 Minutes a Day

Some people think the whole time they are talking to each other. But how often do you speak about things which deepen your partner's understanding? Take 10 minutes a day; I call it the "10 Minute Rule" to talk to your partner about anything other than work, family, home, or relationships. This simple change connects relationships with a new spirit and life.

3. Fall in Love Again every Week

Spontaneous dates are fantastic, but the fact is we are busy and sometimes spend little time with our loved ones. Keep your relationship healthy with a date once a week: eating out, watching a movie, dancing, an art show, and yoga as a couple, whatever. Take turns planning. Studies show women are more excited and have more libido when they're away from home, with kids, and doing housework. See what happens when you reserve your local hotel for a night and ask a relative or family member to see the children and pets.

4. Change Yourself and Grow Together

Your love affair is a living being that needs food to grow and develop. The best way to maintain it is to fill it with change. As with fertilizers for a plant, you introduce relationship changes as an essential part of couples' happiness. The changes may be small, but you need to change the routine so that he or she straightens up and notices. Switching roles: If he's always making dinner reservations, let them do it. Or break off routines: Play work and have fun together, like visiting a museum or a nearby tourist spot. Or try something new: Take part in a water ski event, or make a meditation retreat.

5. Be a Caregiver

One of the three things couples need to be in a happy relationship is support (the other two needs are calm and Intimacy). First, find out what kind of help your partner wants, then give it to them often and consistently.

6. Find a healthy Way to Communicate

Communication skills keep couples to stay together and thrive. This means that not only are you asking your partner what he needs, but you are also telling your partner what you need. It means checking back regularly to determine which stressors in your partner's life are raising their ugly heads and learning how to fight fair without offending, embarrassing, or bogging the kitchen.

7. Have constructive Conversations

If you can't speak to them, you cannot feel a bond with anyone. Do you feel deeply connected to the neighbor you are addressing the weather with? It isn't very sure. But if you paused and learned about their life or personal beliefs, you would develop a relationship with them.

8. Be present

When you're with someone, stick with that person. Don't send text messages on your phone or pay attention to anything that is happening around you. Focus on who you are with and what you are saying. You will realize that you are paying attention and moving back and forth, which improves the relationship for both of you.

9. Be Open to Different Views of Love

Be open to various expressions of love. Finding love in smaller gestures helps you see warmth and happiness in more things in life. In no time, you will find yourself showing your Love in different ways too.

10. Change Your Beliefs about Love and the World

Don't be closed off when it comes to Love and the world. When you are locked in, you will be harder for love to find. Keep your mind and heart open. Love people, no matter their attitudes towards you.

Withholding love will not change anyone for the better; it will only bill you for the worst by making you appear selfish and stingy. Thank those around you.

Conclusion

I told you that I would explain anxiety and get into detail about how anxiety affects relationships. You've not only learned how common anxiety is but how it can negatively affect your life and your relationships. Together, we went through the external and internal causes of anxiety and what type of questions you need to manage your anxiety.

You learned about anxious attachment styles that help you understand if you're anxious or secure. You know techniques to help you rise above an anxious attachment style and reach secure attachment. While this won't happen quickly, every step you take will feel like an improvement in your life and your relationship.

Jealousy is one of the primary ties to anxiety. It's normal to have a little jealousy in your relationship, but it can quickly spiral out of control if you have anxiety. Jealousy is a powerful emotion that makes you feel you need to control your partner. You need to tell them who they can and can't talk to if they can visit with their friends, and cause you to make rules that they have to follow. Jealousy can become so powerful that it takes over your mind and emotions. This leads you down a dangerous path in your relationship where you become manipulative or abusive. Fortunately, there are a lot of strategies you can focus on to help ease your jealousy. You've learned what you need to do to take control of your jealousy before it takes control of you and your relationship.

Anxiety stems from where you can continue working toward building up your relationship. This doesn't mean that you're no longer working through your issues. It merely means that you're starting to take control. You'll spend years talking to a therapist or focusing on management techniques. You'll be working on these techniques and focusing on strategies to build your trust and strengthen your relationship at the same time. Trust is one of the main foundations of any relationship. It's also a significant tie to your anxiety issues as you struggle to trust people, even the ones who love and care for you the most.

You also learned several secrets to a happy and long-lasting relationship with little anxiety attached. These secrets are meant for you to bring into your relationship so you can start strengthening your connection, communication, and other foundational building blocks. But, even with these secrets, you might still need to look at therapy. First, I understand it's hard for some people to admit that they need therapy. Unfortunately, many people feel that it makes them weak or a failure. But this is not how anyone should see therapy. Facing the fact that you need to see a counselor improve your life and your partner's life, your family, and your relationship is one of the greatest strengths that you possess. You should never be ashamed when you walk into a counselor's office.

Finally, you learned that no matter how hard you try, anxiety will rear its ugly head. It will come back and try to haunt you as the little voice in your head grows louder. It's up to you to take a break and understand why your anxiety is knocking on your door.

One of the most critical insights that I want you to hold in your heart is that you're a healthy person with high potential. You have your whole life in your hands, and it's up to you to take the steps you need to so you can reach your goals. You need to take a stand against your anxiety, so you learn how to manage it. Even when it seems impossible, trust me when I write that you have everything you need to manage your anxiety. Believe in yourself because you already took one significant step in the right direction. Be proud of where you are now, and continue to look forward.

Part Three:

The Marriage Counseling
Workbook

CHAPTER 1:

The Marriage Basics

When it comes to getting married, only a few people are sure what they are getting themselves into. We have our hopes, expectations, and dreams of what marriage indeed looks like. When we watch some of the movies starts, we like, we think that the kinds of weddings they show on TV are what it is like in real life.

Let me tell you something. You have no idea what marriage is until you are there!

Here Are some of the Secrets I Can Tell You Will Strengthen Your Marriage if You Pay Attention to Them;

Secret 1 Marriage Is more about Intimacy than Sex

If you ask anyone that is single and planning to get married what marriage is about, they will tell you it is about sex. While there is so much value you draw from getting married to your partner as far as your sexual relationship, the truth is that a good marriage is built on intimacy. This is the only route you are going to enjoy good sex and not the other way around.

Secret 2 Marriage Uncovers Self-Centeredness but Also Cultivates Selflessness

Confessions, I didn't realize how selfish I was until I got married to my wife. One year down the line, my selfishness was out in the light. I could choose what restaurant we would eat, who gets to clean up, what movie we will watch, and who gets the remote. It was even shocking that each time we argued, my wife would apologize first even if I was the one at fault.

Learn to place your spouse's needs before your own if you are going to make it last. This is how you start learning the true meaning of being selfless. Trust me, even though this is a hard lesson to learn, it is a beautiful reminder of God's selflessness when He gave His all so that you and I can have it all in abundance.

Secret 3 Oneness Means Being one

The truth is, when we get into marriage, we stop being "me" and become "us." We stop having things that are "mine," and we view everything as "ours." You have to care for everything as though they were not just yours but also belonged to the person you love most.

Secret 4 At Certain Points, You Will Be disappointed

This is one of the most challenging realities that most couples find it hard to believe. You must be aware of your spouse's humanity and yours too. However, it is interesting that this reality does not hit home sooner until you are disappointed.

You must choose to embrace the grace of God so that every hurt and wound pave the way for forgiveness and restoration. Each injury should serve as a constant reminder of our need to love profoundly and better each time.

Secret 5 You Must Learn the Meaning of Forgiveness whether You Like It or Not

The fact that you will get hurt means that you have to embrace the reality of learning the essence of forgiveness. One lesson that you must know is that forgiveness comes not just because your partner deserves it but also because it whelms from a heart that understands how much forgiveness we had received even when we least deserved it.

Secret 6 Marriage Will Cost You

When you are in the glory of marriage, the truth is that you will lose a part of yourself. In other words, you exchange a portion of who you are for the sake of taking up a little bit of who your partner is.

In short, you learn the essence of giving and taking. In marriage, you know to let go of the things that do not matter to you at all. Eventually, you realize that what you have given is far much less than what you ultimately receive.

Trust me; love is good, just like that!

Secret 7 Love Is a Series of Decision and Not a Feeling

Before you got married, the chances are that you did not understand the intense feelings that you felt. Suddenly, you start realizing that you cannot trust your feelings because there are days when you don't like your spouse, and most days, you just can't let him go.

The actual test of love is what you do when you feel that you don't like your spouse. Understand that marriage is about choosing to love your partner even when you don't want to. You are choosing to give your all into serving them because you committed to them, the world, and God that you would love them "for better or for worse." It is about you always choosing your spouse instead of yourself.

That is what real life means!

Secret 8 Marriage Requires that You Learn how to Communicate

We have mentioned before that one of the essential building blocks of marriage is compelling, transparent, and honest communication. What matters the most is what you would do about it. How will you choose to communicate to them how you feel?

In short, marriage is about you continue communicating with your spouse, your values, beliefs, opinions, and feelings. It is about not fearing to ask the tough questions, tell the hard truth, or even respond to difficult problems. It serves as a lifeline between you and your spouse.

Secret 9 Marriage Is Not the end of Your Destination

When you are still dating, it is often easy to look at marriage as your grand finale! It is that thing that you have been dreaming about since you were a little girl or boy. It is what you have lived for all your life, and finally, it is here. The following thing you think of when you get married is, "Now what?"

The truth is that your purpose and passion will supersede the relationship you have with your partner. God will use your relationship and the love between you and your spouse for the glory of His name. Your marriage is not the end of everything. Instead, it is just the beginning of the many more blessings he has in store for you.

Secret 10 Marriage Offers You a Glimpse of So Much more

God has so much more in store for you. Realize that there is a reason why God uses the institution of marriage when talking about the love He has for the church.

There is no single relationship you will have that will compare to that intimacy exchanged through marriage here on earth. In other words, it is through marriage that God keeps making us be more of Him.

CHAPTER 2:

Communication

Ensuring that you have open communication with your partner will help you build a long-lasting and happy relationship. By contrast, people with poor communication skills are much more likely to have unresolved fights and unhealthy relationships.

Self-Disclosure

We get scared when we think about sharing or revealing a secret about ourselves. This triggers feelings of guilt, shame, and fear. When you share the vulnerabilities with a stranger or someone you don't know very well, this can potentially lead to more insecurities. Without meaning to, the other person can challenge our core beliefs, which can trigger anxiety or depression. Sharing your vulnerability with your closest friends or your partner can be liberating, and it's a great way to strengthen your bond.

Rewards of Self-Disclosure

Self-disclosure can lead to long-lasting relationships, reduced anxiety, and elimination of the feeling of abandonment. Some of the many benefits of self-disclosure are listed below.

- **Eliminate feelings of guilt** — Chronic feelings of guilt can change a person's entire life. But keeping all the parts of yourself that you feel ashamed of hidden is impossible to sustain. Remember that imperfections are a part of life, and when you start hiding things from the people you love, you will begin the ensuing of shame and guilt can take over your whole life.

- **Improve communication** — When you open up to your partner, chances are you will inspire them to do the same. This will naturally lead to better communication between you. Make an effort to share your true self with your partner. You will find yourself sharing the most intimate details about your life and living happily together in no time.

- **More intimate relationships** — Disclosing personal information and sharing your feelings will help you form closer bonds with the people you love. This will lead to more meaningful interactions with those around you. Indeed, a welcome change from the unsatisfying and shallow relationship you might have had in the past.

- **Increased self-knowledge** — We're all pretty well-aware of all the secrets we keep. So, you might be wondering how sharing them with your partner can increase knowledge about yourself. The truth is, when you don't share your feelings with anyone, you tend to make assumptions that have no real basis in facts. Moreover, going over and over your secrets in your mind will never provide you with any total closure. Sharing this information with your partner will give you a new and fresh perspective, and you will be eager to find out even more information that can help you solve these issues.

Listening Skills

Listening skills are probably the most crucial step to bridge the communication gap between you and your partner. When someone feels indeed heard, they tend to feel empowered, loved, supported, and understood. Your listening skill is essential if you want your partner to feel loved and cared for.

But before we talk about something called "active listening," which is our goal, we need to show you the difference between really listening and pseudo-listening.

Pseudo-Listening vs. Real Listening

Pseudo-listening is a concept that we should all be aware of. As you may have guessed, pseudo-listening is only half-listening to what the other person says, not paying much attention. One sign of pseudo-listening is when you start thinking about how to reply to what the other person is saying before they're done talking. Another is when you engage in other activities, such as looking at your phone when talking. This can lead to many issues since people who have this habit have trouble keeping successful relationships. They're unable to fully process the information that other people share with them, which can be harmful to the relationship. Not feeling heard might also trigger feelings of anxiety in someone with fearful or preoccupied attachment styles.

Listening Blocks

Numerous things can hinder your capacity to remain focused on what the other person is trying to say to you. Suppose you've even been in that situation yourself. In that case, you probably remember that your attention was mostly focused on what you were going to say about yourself than what other people were saying. Maybe you practiced your speech in your mind over and over to avoid making mistakes, or we just too anxious about speaking publicly. Whatever the cause, listening blocks can only have a damaging effect on your relationship.

Active Listening

If you feel that your communication skills require some work and improve your relationships, you need to listen to your daily routine actively. Knowing about pseudo-listening and listening blocks is an excellent first step, but good communication requires additional work. When you start to listen to other people truly, you will be able to respond more insightfully, in a way that makes them feel you dully support them.

Step 1: Paraphrasing

Paraphrasing is expressing the meaning of what someone else has said using different words. A practical example might help to make the concept clearer.

Person A: I don't think my partner cares about me anymore. They never reply to my messages or calls anymore.

Person B: So, you feel neglected because your partner isn't talking to you as often as they used to?

In paraphrasing, you use your own words to help you focus on what the other person is saying and to show that you understand the meaning they're trying to convey.

Step 2: Clarifying

Consider clarifying as an addition to paraphrasing. In this step, you will ask questions until you understand what the other person is trying to communicate. Look at the example above once more. Notice how Person B not only paraphrased Person A's statement but also turned it into a question? This is the idea behind clarification.

With this process, you will gather more information and know what message the other person conveys.

Step 3: Feedback

The third and final step is providing feedback. After you fully absorb and comprehend the information presented to you, it's time to share your thoughts. Once you have assimilated their words, you offer a message back, communicating that you have listened to the speaker and want to engage in a meaningful dialogue.

The key to providing meaningful feedback is to offer a message free of judgment. When the speaker receives positive feedback from you, they know that you understand their side of the story and feel empowered. This will also lead to less anxiety in the relationship.

There are three basic rules you should follow when giving feedback. The feedback should be honest (even if it's painful), it should be immediate, and it should have a supportive tone.

Expressing Your Needs

Expressing your needs may seem like an easy thing to do, but it can be complicated. Many people just aren't used to asking for attention or saying their needs. Yet others may think they don't need anything from other people.

The prominent problem people face is that we have become more alienated from the concept of expressing our needs. Many people have probably gone years without it. We might get the urge to communicate our needs to our friends, family members, or romantic partner, but we often smother and ignore it. This is most likely because we fear rejection, which could increase the problems in the relationship.

CHAPTER 3:

Intimacy

T hings may start to feel a bit dull, and sex drives may not be as strong as they used to be. Give time for a sexual relationship with your partner by trying new things, communicating about personal desires, and playing fun games.

Increase Couple Intimacy

When you become progressively more comfortable with someone, it can take away some of the mystery. This is because there is no longer the excitement of getting to know a person, and having everything you do together be brand new. At the beginning of a relationship, you are eager to have sex with each other because the other person is unique and hot and a novelty of sorts. As you get used to them, it can be easy to lose those feelings and settle into the comfortability of everything (like their body or your routine).

Getting to this point in your relationship is fun and comforting in its way, and is different from, but in some ways better than, the early stages. From a sexual perspective, though, we don't want the coming of this stage of your relationship to bring with it the end of exciting sex life.

If you are a long-term or married couple, you have likely tried every one of the classic sex positions together from missionary to 69. You have probably also developed a routine of your favorite parts and the order in which you do them by now. Start having sex casually before getting together romantically, or you may have begun having sex when you became a couple. Either way, the beginning of any relationship comes with a lot of uncharted territories. You are exploring a new person's entire body- inside and out, and letting them see all of yours. Of course, this can be nerve-wracking. There will be some positions and sexual activities that you won't be entirely comfortable doing with this person yet, even if you have done them before with someone else. There are certain positions you can stick to that are more comfortable at the beginning of a relationship, and that is best for getting to know someone's body and what they like. These positions serve us well when we are newly having sex with a person and are looking for the best way to help each other orgasm. This stage of discovery, however, is something that we want to return to every so often. We want to rediscover the person's body and what they like as if it is the first time, we explore it. People's desires change, and their bodies change. It is vital to continue to know how to pleasure your partner as they grow and change, and to expect the same from them for yourself.

Importance of Spicing Up Your Sex Life

The primary importance of spicing up your sex life is to increase intimacy between you and your partner. Not only does this help your sex life become more fun and exciting, but it also improves the communication and bond between you and your partner. We will look at how you can maintain intimacy with your partner and achieve a greater intimacy level and will do for your relationship.

Intimacy is crucial between two people when part of a couple, especially in the bedroom. Intimacy is what brings you close and keeps you close. Firstly, we will look at what intimacy means and the different types of intimacy that exist. There are different types of intimacy, and here I will outline them for you before digging deeper into the intimacy between couples. Intimacy, in a general sense, is defined as mutual openness and vulnerability between two people. Therefore, it is not only reserved for romantic relationships. Intimacy can also be present in other types of close relationships like friendships or family relationships. Below, I will outline the different forms of intimacy.

Emotional Intimacy

Emotional intimacy is the ability to express oneself maturely and openly, leading to a deeply personal connection between people. It is also the ability to respond maturely and openly when someone expresses themselves to you by saying things like "I'm sorry" or "I love you too."

This open and vulnerable dialogue leads to an emotional connection. There must be a mutual willingness to be vulnerable and honest, with more in-depth thoughts and feelings for a deep personal connection to form. This is where this type of emotional intimacy comes from.

Intellectual Intimacy

Intellectual intimacy is a kind of intimacy that involves discussing and sharing thoughts and opinions on intellectual matters. They gain fulfillment and feelings of closeness with the other person. For example, if you discuss politics with someone you deem to be an intellectual equal, you may find that you feel a closeness with them as you share your thoughts and opinions and connect on an intellectual level. Many people find intellect and brains to be sexy in a partner!

Shared Interests and Activities

This form of intimacy is less well-known, but it is also considered a form of intimacy. When you share activities with another person, you both enjoy and are passionate about it. This creates a sense of connection. For example, when you cook together or travel together. These shared experiences give you memories to share, leading to bonding and intimacy (openness and vulnerability). This type of connection is usually present in friendships, familial relationships, and, more importantly, in romantic relationships. Being able to share interests and activities leads to a closeness that can be defined as intimacy.

Physical Intimacy

Physical intimacy is what most people think of when they hear the term "intimacy," as it is the type of intimacy that includes sex and all activities related to sex. It also involves other non-sexual types of physical contact, such as hugging and kissing. Physical intimacy can be found in close friendships or familial relationships where hugging and kisses on the cheek are common, but it is most often found in romantic relationships.

Physical intimacy is the type of intimacy involved when people are trying to make each other orgasm. Physical intimacy is almost always required for orgasm. Physical intimacy doesn't necessarily mean that you are in love with the person you are having sex with; it just means that you are doing something intimate with another person physically.

It is also possible to be intimate with yourself. While this begins with the emotional intimacy of self-awareness, it also involves the physical closeness of masturbation and physical self-exploration. I define sexual, the physical intimacy of the self as being in touch with the parts of yourself physically that you would not usually be in touch with if you are a woman, your breasts, clitoris, vagina, and anus. Suppose you are a man, your testicles, your penis, your anus. Being physically intimate with yourself allows you to have more fulfilling sex, more fulfilling orgasms, and a more fulfilling overall relationship with your body. Being in charge of your own body while it is in another person's hands is very important. This is why masturbation is such a pivotal element to physical intimacy.

CHAPTER 4:

Finance

Money-it's probably a couple's most challenging subject to discuss calmly. It is often identified as the leading cause of marital discord. Pairs with an unbalanced perception of this product will suffer from tension, conflict, and emotional damage. However, parents who are unable to overcome money issues friendly also raise children with irrational financial attitudes. But is money meant to cause inconsistencies in your home? Not necessary. Not necessarily. On the contrary, money discussions can strengthen your marriage bond. It's all about how you look at money and how you talk to your spouse about it. Why is money a source of peace and marriage at once?

Many conflicts involving money in the home frequently rely instead of cash or credit on trust or fear. For instance, a husband who demands his wife to account for every hundred she spends may say that he fears that the woman can handle family finances. Likewise, the wife, who worries that her husband saves too little, may express her fear that a future event may cause financial harm to her family.

Then there's another challenge-the background of the couple. Consider the hypothetical husband I'm going to call Johnny. He is from a family where his dad was an alcoholic and a smoking band. The dad was often out of work for long stretches. As a result, the family often had to deal with simple things in the house. Based on that background, Johnny developed a real fear of debt or cash flow. Sometimes this fear makes him irrational about money matters with his wife. The wife is from a family, on the other hand, where money was well handled. Of course, she doesn't have the many hang-ups Johnny has about money. Often these gaps lead to tensions.

Learn to Talk calmly about Money

At such moments, emotions would be substantial, making peaceful and constructive conversations almost impossible. This can common the disputes arising from hot emotions and incomprehension. And what can you talk about? Why don't you trust your wife how your parents' attitude to the money could have influenced you? Try to understand how your partner's background could have affected her or his philosophy that one regard. Such discussions may seem awkward, going to depend on the personality of yours and the environment. But if it contributes to home peace, won't you confront it?

Agree as to how Income Is to Be considered

If both you and your spouse earn money, be careful not to claim individual independence. In the family, it does not promote peace. Honor each other by revealing your income and significant expenses. Hiding your income or your high costs can undermine your confidence and harm your relationship. This doesn't mean you have to ask your friend before you pay for a bottle of soda. That could threaten the precious independence that every individual wants reasonably. Yet you illustrate that by reporting larger purchases, you respect your partner and his opinion. In this regard, both of you can agree on an amount each of you can spend without informing the other, whether this is $20, $200, or any other figure. And always ask your partner if you want to spend more than that.

Try Budgeting

It also helps to erase suspicions that either partner has wasted unnecessary money. Facts and figures are difficult to argue about. A family budget should not be as complicated as a national budget. A straightforward calculation of a household's total income, a listing of payroll fixed and variable costs, and judgment on what proportion of payment should be saved after bills are paid. Through keeping a list of actual expenses for many months, you can further refine the family budget and equate them with the existing account. Change your lifestyle to keep your family from falling into debt if necessary.

Distribution Roles

Considering each other's strengths and weaknesses, determine who will take care of what responsibility at home. Here, there is no hard and quick rule. The husband takes care of finances in some households, and the wife takes care of this duty in others. This is what works for your family. The goal is that both you and your partner work as a team (for you!). Besides, you may agree to swap roles sometimes, to learn better what each other does.

Your money conversations don't have to stifle one another's passion. Open discussions on money may be between husband and wife to enhance the love connection. As couples talk about how they want to spend money, they share their goals and desires and, at the same time, affirm their marriage commitment. They respect each other's opinions and sentiments when they consult each other before making large purchases. If they require the relative freedom to spend a certain amount without consultation, they show mutual trust. These are the characteristics of a genuinely loving relationship. Don't they value more than cash? Why argue?

CHAPTER 5:

Family Structure

Relationships are complicated things, even the relationships that exist between family members. To have the best possible relationship with your spouse, your children, or any other family members, you have to play a constant game of trial and error to find out what doesn't work and what does. Over time, relationships grow more substantial, and when you make mistakes, you learn valuable lessons.

All about Family Relationships

The most important part of a healthy family is the relationships that exist between each of the members. Because of these distractions, you may have grown comfortable living in solitude, although the rest of your family shares the same home with you. In fact, for some families, they first have to go through horrible events like accidents or divorce before they realize how meaningful their relationships are.

Learn how to prioritize and nurture your relationships to make them stronger. When this improvement in relationships starts with you, the rest of your family members will also feel encouraged to follow suit. Soon, you will realize that your family has grown closer, and you share more profound relationships. But before you can do this, you should recognize the signs that your family is undergoing problems. To work on making your relationships better, you must deal with existing issues first. Some of the most common issues that cause rifts in your relationships are:

When One Member Has a strong Need for Dominance and Power

Usually, this is felt by one of the parents, although children may feel this too (especially teenagers). All families have dominant members and less dominant members. But if one of the dominant members wants everyone else to follow everything they say, that will cause some tension. For instance, if one of the parents gets involved in a conflict with another family member, it might upset them. When this happens, the parent might exert his control and power by ordering everyone else to cut-off communications with that family member. Naturally, if the family member involved is close to the rest of the family, they might not want to cut-off communication.

If you have one such member in your family, you should have a conversation with them.

When One Family Member Makes Others Feel exhausted

Certain people can make others feel depleted or exhausted, even without trying too hard. For instance, if your spouse finds parenting too tricky, and they become incredibly pessimistic. Even the smallest things set them off, and they end up taking out their frustrations on you or, worse, on your children. This is another issue that you have to deal with first before starting your minimalist journey.

Lack of Loyalty

Sometimes, when family issues get too overwhelming, one spouse tries to find comfort in another person instead of dealing with the home issues. Lack of loyalty may also manifest when a teenager chooses their friends or boy/girlfriend over their family. Generally, though, a lack of loyalty happens because there is also a lack of communication between family members. Be brave enough to reach out, especially when you feel like an issue is troubling one of your family members. Loyalty doesn't just happen — you should love and nurture each other so that you will all feel loyalty and trust towards each other no matter what challenges come your way.

Financial Issues

Fortunately, this is one problem that you can deal with through minimalism. When you focus on material things (including money), it won't be that much of a problem anymore.

Abusive Family Members

Sadly, so many people have been abused physically, emotionally, verbally, or psychologically by their family members. The effects of abuse don't go away smoothly, and some even carry the repercussions of these experiences until they grow up. If needed, ask for professional help to deal with this issue.

CHAPTER 6:

Parenting

Parenting is a game-changer to all marriages. In many ways, it can change the relationship dynamic for the better or worse, depending on the specific set of circumstances. In television commercials featuring baby-shower cards, diapers, and a litany of baby products, parenting and marriage are depicted as pure bliss and effortless. Your relatives will sell you a story about how babies are a heaven-sent bundle of happiness — and they are — but they skip the hard work that goes into making it all work! Of course, it is essential to love our children. But it is crucial to be alive to what parenting does to marriages. There is no reason that loving your child and working on your marriage should be mutually exclusive. A happy marriage almost always means a happy baby. Marriage happiness, sustainability, and worth are liked at the hip with parenting.

Can Parenting Be Used to Strength Marriages?

It is not easy. It is difficult. But marriage can be used to sweeten your marriage, make it more robust and long-lasting! Most people view parenting as a collection of stressors that will make your life miserable and probably accelerate the end of your relationship with your spouse. However, with the right touch, parenting can be the glue that holds you together. In this regard, it will benefit your relationship and the well-being of the kid(s).

All you can do to leverage parenting in improving your relationship within a marriage is to put your relationship first. Recognizing that your marriage is a work in progress goes a long way to cementing your commitment towards bolstering your bonds. Working on your differences consistently also helps strengthen your relationship's foundations while ironing out disagreements before they become more significant issues.

A focus on appreciating each other while minimizing criticism is essential in sweetening your relationship. Communication is the underlying foundation of a relationship. Maintaining the bidirectional flow of information, opinions, views, and perspectives are necessary, retaining the enthusiasm to sustain a relationship of married spouses with a kid(s).

Using parenting as a tool to improve your relationship quality and sustainability needs a deliberate effort targeting parenting dynamics. Understanding the expected disruptions to the relationship parenting brings will help you be better prepared. It also means that you are better equipped to harness the parenting changes and work for your relationship.

Learning about parenting and preparing for the shifts it brings should include both spouses. This process must be collaborative because both of you will need the knowledge and skills to maneuver through the impending changes.

Secondly, a concerted approach is likely to succeed in maintaining a working and significant relationship. When both of you put in the work, you are susceptible to shoulder the burden equitably. Although parenting cannot biologically be equitable, it creates a sense that the husband is supportive of the wife during this period.

The challenge facing most couples going into marriage is that they are not prepared for parenting disruptions. They are not ready for the upending of their lives they face after the baby is born, and parenting begins. As a result, parenting becomes overwhelming, physically, and emotionally. This leads to a surge in conflicts and an increase in the likelihood of divorce or unhappy marriages/relationships.

Use Parenting as a Platform to Build a stronger and long-lasting Relationship and Marriage:

- **Talk About the Certainties and Uncertainties Ahead**

  Talking about uncertainties does not make them any more confident. However, it will help you be emotionally prepared and sure of yourself when navigating through parenting moments and circumstances.

  It is also essential to plan and ventilate some particular issues, such as splitting errands and household chores. It is essential to talk about where the income of the family will come from. In this case, it is crucial to answering the following questions: Who will be the breadwinner? And who is going to stay at home rearing the child?

Talk about the day-care option. Establish who will get your baby to the day-care center and who will get him/her back. Explore the issue of a babysitter, the budget for this option, and plan your lives around what you agree. Figure out how night shift duties will be split, who will wash or sterilize the breast pump and bottles daily. Figure out the shopping schedule, cooking plan, and cleaning chores.

These details seem small and harmless. But without figuring out the division of labor regarding these aspects, they might contribute to frustration, stress, and depression. If left unsorted, they can gnaw away at the relationship.

- **Focus on the Downside of Parenthood with the View of Avoiding Its Pitfalls on the Marriage**

  Maintaining a positive and hopeful perception of parenting is important for new fathers and mothers. But it is vital to guard against lofty expectations shattered by the reality of fatherhood and motherhood.

  Yes, babies offer immense joy, and they bring a lot of happiness to a marriage. They also carry an uptick in physical and emotional exertions that can take their toll on the relationship. Bathing the baby, feeding, entertaining, and changing the baby

24 hours a day and 7 hours a week are demanding chores. All couples should be emotionally and physically prepared for such demands before they begin their roles as parents. Focusing on and talking about the downside(s) of parenting is essential in marriage. It will help you to cope with the changes and disruptions to your lives. It is okay to talk about your fatigue, frustrations, and even anger with your spouse. Ensure, to be honest with your partner regarding these issues and also maintaining a supportive stance. Feeling anger, frustration, and fatigue does not mean that you are a terrible parent. It is crucial to admit these emotions and focus on working together to resolve them within the marriage. This approach helps in disarming these emotions and thus prevents them from negatively affecting your relationship.

- **Maintain Honesty about Gains and Losses**

In many instances, parenting will lead to some gains and losses. For example, you have gained the baby of your dreams. He/she melts your heart every time you see them. However, you cannot avoid feeling sad and empty because of the loss of your typical sex life. For the mother, you lost your sleek pre-baby size 8s and replaced them with elastic-waist jeans. Most new parents typically complain, silently, about the disruption to their lives occasioned by the baby and their parenting duties and responsibilities. These complaints and silent resentment cause the marital distance to widen. In some extreme instances, it can lead to shame and a decline in self-esteem. For example,

144 | P a g .

a new daddy might feel replaced by the baby in his spouse's life and affection. The mother might be frustrated and even sad about how parenting (pregnancy, nursing, and the rigors of childcare) has transformed her body. These feelings are normal among new parents. Sharing such feelings of loss, shame, or disruption is vital in dealing with parenting's emotional toll. Maintaining honesty about these issues with your partner helps you to feel better and strengthen your bond as a couple.

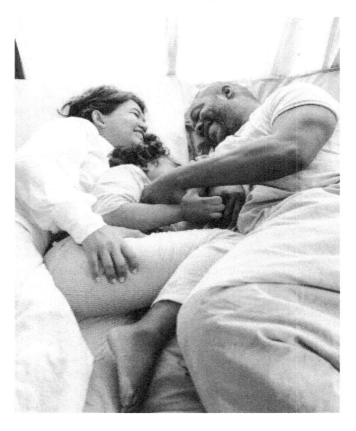

CHAPTER 7:

Extended Family

In-Laws Controversies

Much of the families struggle with in-law's issues at some stage. First, you might believe your in-laws are not helping you, or your spouse is too insensitive. So, they have a view about all the things that go of where you're living and how you feed your kids. Getting disputes with in-laws of yours does not imply you are part of an unhealthy relationship. It's analogous to fighting.

The controversy should not spoil a relationship. And somehow, they're likely to do something wrong. But the same goes out for the problems of an in-law. What matters is how they cope with those issues. Here's how equilibrated partners handle their in-laws:

- **Healthy Couples Put Effort to Maintain a good Relationship with Their In-Laws**

    They understand the position that their in-laws have in their partner's life. They manage things publicly. They are a component of social roles. They require connections to their families from their in-laws.

In certain words, they make an effort, even though they don't generally agree, respect the families' nuances, traditions, or rituals, or even look ahead to the future while being together.

- **Healthy Couples Don't Take It on a personal Basis**

With familiar and complicated human feelings, a happy couple can recognize and deal with the fact that their parents are also human beings. They're trying to figure out where they came from because they are empathizing.

- **Healthy Couples Get to Know Their In-Laws Are Unique People**

Good households deal with their in-laws and recognize that in specific ways, they are unique people.

The communities still have their existence. Good couples realize culture is not wrong or bad, just unique.

- **Healthy Couples Have Their Perfect Boundaries with Their In-Laws**

They should have open conversations with their spouses about their interests and create a plan that they both rely on. For instance: Your partner is okay with an unannounced one coming from his mother.

You don't. And you believe you can call family members in advance to make sure it's a fun moment to go over.

- **Healthy Couples how to Maintain the Difference between Their Spouse and Their In-Laws**

Mom can be disrespectful and critical of an individual, for example. Still, a successful couple understands that her behavior does not portray how the guy feels about the items she focuses on.

- **Healthy Couples Distinct Their Relationship from Their In-Laws**

As they're not partnering with them, regardless of how complicated or disagreeable their in-laws can be. Though the in-laws are incredibly challenging to deal with, satisfied individuals give their partner a particular opportunity to succeed. They can say, "I love you" or perform a sweet gesture.

- **Healthy Couples Know how to Maintain Their Communication**

To deal with in-laws is term sorting. Therefore, they dream about their places.

They are careful. They have complete respect for each other's feelings.

Tips for Dealing with In-Laws

Five more guidelines for coping with the in-laws are here:

- **Setting Your Boundaries**

   Defines the boundaries that you wish to arrange for your in-laws. For example, if your mother-in-law takes over your kitchen every time she comes, talk about it to your spouse. Then talk with her about this same problem in a polite but still straightforward manner.

- **Take deep Breaths for Getting Relax**

   Take a break to relax while you're about to hit a breakpoint. Find a quiet spot, like a shower room, or have a walk. When relaxing, reflect on your in-law's good qualities, such as just enjoying our family, also note that you cannot influence them or alter them. Your in-laws and they are part of your life, are meaningful to your family. It is up to all of you to find a way to make the time with extended family as fun as possible.

- **Remember Your In-Laws Are People**

   They are like you. They have interests, fears, anxieties, and thoughts. Do not treat them as caretakers, just like every other person you slowly become familiar with.

- **Remember, It's Just an Opinion**

  If your mother-in-law recommends feeding your child with a different diet, take note that you don't have to accept it, defend it out of the presence or view it as your criticism. Although we can't help but speak with an in-law, we can legislate how we hear them.

- **Respect Your Spouse's Attachments**

  As it helps to view the husband's commitment to his relatives as something that should be valued. For starters, if your husband's regular calls to his father are worth able to him, then recognizing and acknowledging that is valuable to you.

CHAPTER 8:

Build Trust

Fidelity in a marriage isn't just sexual; it's emotional, physical, psychological, and spiritual. When you trust your marriage partner, you are saying I can trust who you are. It means that you respect and understand your partner's actions and decisions, that you believe your partner is reliable in their word and predictably safe in their choices. Trust is the ability to coexist peacefully with the unknown and act with incomplete information because you've filled in the gaps with tacit knowledge that feels safe, intimate, and understandable.

Trust requires a mystical blend of intimate knowledge of another person, and a willingness to accept that another person can never fully, wholly be known.

In marriage, trust is an essential ingredient for success. Breaches of trust are like holes in the bottom of a boat:

Whether the water seeps in through hundreds of tiny rot spots or gushes through one gaping hole, without repair, that boat is going to sink. (But you could always decide to get on another boat together!)

Build Trust with Time-Outs

Despite your best intentions, the train of communication will still derail. Sometimes it's a spectacular crash; other times, you feel the wheels start to rattle, and you know to slow down. That's what a time-out does — it slows things down so that you can both get back on the track of connection, mutual understanding, and alignment. Pausing a problematic conversation is also a way to build and maintain trust in your marriage. It says to your partner, "What we're talking about is important, but I'm having trouble listening with my heart. Trust me to take a break and come back when I'm ready."

Here Are the Step-by-Step Do's and Don'ts of Taking a Time-Out:

a. **Frame the Need for a Time-Out in Terms of Your Own Experience, Rather than Blaming Your Partner**

- Don't blame your partner by saying something like, "You're getting worked up. Have a break to calm down."

- Do acknowledge the helpfulness of a time-out for yourself. For example: "I'm feeling overwhelmed. What you're saying is important, but I'm having trouble listening to what you're saying. I need a break, and then we can try again."

b. **Engage in healthy Self-soothing**

- Don't numb or escalate (that is, don't avoid or minimize your feelings, use substances, shame or blame yourself for needing a break, complain to others, or shut down).

- Do relax and recover. For example, meditate, take a shower or a bath, exercise, or go for a walk, write in a journal, read, or watch a funny TV show.

c. **Revisit the Conversation in Your Mind to Prepare for another Try**

- Don't skip this step. Couples who only self-soothe but don't engage in the work of perspective-taking end up rehashing the same fight over and over again. Time-outs are helpful only if you both identify ways you can do better after. Recovery takes active processing.

- Do remember what is essential. Couples are ready to try again for a productive conversation when they've spent the time-out actively processing what happened. What's important is that you're a team, you speak and listen with your heart, and you prevent further damage. Ask yourself questions like, "When I felt triggered, what did I think my partner was trying to say or intending to mean? What triggered my partner? How do I imagine they felt? How can I state my needs differently so my partner can hear me? How can I convey that I understand where my partner is coming from, even if I disagree?"

d. **Try Again**

- Don't assume that you don't need to talk about the conflict because you're feeling better from self-soothing and active processing. Honor the request to try again, and give yourselves the chance to get back to the original issue.

- Do return to the conversation when you're both ready. Bring a more intentional awareness of the skills you've learned, like active listening (see here) or Stop, Drop, Swap (see here). And add in some physical touching this time — remember, it's harder to argue when you're touching!

e. **Interacting with each other during the Time-Out**

You may still need to interact with each other during the break from your difficult conversation. Perhaps you need to get the kids to bed during the time-out or meet friends for brunch. How should you interact with each other during the in-between time? Remember, the time-out is meant to repair a communication derailment, not to do further damage. You can be warm and not ready to talk about the issue at hand. You can process hurt feelings and not punish your partner.

155 | P a g .

- Don't be passive-aggressive, cold, distant, or sarcastic; don't slam doors or sigh heavily.

- Do be respectful, warm, friendly, and kind; maintain small acts of affection, and smile.

Betrayals

Betrayals in marriage take many forms, from affairs to secrets to lies. At its core, a betrayal is a form of disloyalty — an indication that something or someone else has taken priority, preference, or value over the partnership. Betrayal in a marriage is toxic because it signals violations of marriage values like mutuality, respect, and teamwork. Two of the most common forms of betrayal in marriage, besides sexual betrayals, are secrets and lies.

Secrets

Secrets in a marriage can take different forms — perhaps you've started withholding information to avoid a conflict, like when you use cash to pay for something, so there isn't a credit card trail. Or perhaps you're keeping secrets from your partner because you're ashamed of the truth (or what your partner would think about your truth), like when you bought a pack of cigarettes even though you're trying to quit and your partner would be disappointed.

Marriage asks us to be vulnerable and open with our partner and requires us to do our part to create an emotionally safe environment that facilitates such sharing. It asks of one another, "Share your true self with me."

Lies

Consistency and honesty are two fundamental values in a partnership. To build lives together, you need to know that your partner will do what they say and say what they mean, and vice versa. Intentional deception quickly undermines trust in a marriage, no matter if the lies are "white" or "whoppers." Like why we might keep a secret from our partner, a lie can be a way to avoid confrontation. "I didn't tell you because I knew you'd get upset — just like you're doing now!" But lying only compounds the injury; one wound is the complicated truth itself, and the other is the deception that hid that truth. Even those dealing with betrayal on the affair level often hear from my clients that the lying hurts more than the actions.

CHAPTER 9:

Roles and Expectation

You should believe that your partner does not fulfill your emotional needs. However, marriage counselors and psychologists usually believe that only you can satisfy these needs.

It's not meant to be seen as a hollow emotional container packed with your partner. You've got to take responsibility for your results. The best way to do this is to recognize and fulfill the needs of your partner first.

To Meet What Your Spouse Needs

Both men and women have very different needs. Learning to consider and fulfill your partner's needs can be difficult, but it is vital to creating a successful marriage. If the adversary is granted a foothold, it will devastate a few purely because of their unmet needs and desires.

In a variety of instances, married couples tend to struggle to fulfill their partners' needs. Satisfying your emotional desires requires putting the needs of your partner ahead of your own.

Having a proper understanding of your partner's emotional needs is one of the keys to success in a long-term, engaged relationship. Not meeting all of your partner's needs is not your responsibility. If you want your spouse to take action to meet your needs magically, you are asking for them to change.

Instead, be direct and frank to your partner. Ask what you need. Would you like change, understanding, or compatibility? Whatever you need, requesting it directly will significantly improve your chances of getting it.

Show Your Spouse that You Care

This is where the need for reciprocity comes into play. Time and again, show your spouse that you appreciate and care for them. Reminding your partner that you know your life is better because they are in is very motivating and loving.

Kindness Goes a long Way

It doesn't matter what the act of kindness is. The vital thing is that your spouse knows that they are valued, that you know what they want and need, and that you are willing to provide it without prompting.

These efforts to learn and offer are the keys to a successful marriage and relationship, and eventually, fulfill your own needs.

Take Responsibility for Yourself

Understand that you are in a relationship to bond with your spouse, share events large or small, and build a life together.

Prepare for disappointment since both parties cannot always satisfy each other. Expecting another person to meet our needs entirely is asking too much of anyone.

Expectations are grueling that all humans are fallible and have their wants and needs. This is unlikely to change in your own space or that of anyone else.

Don't see where your spouse needs to change. Look where you need to change. Don't have expectations of your spouse. In case you have expectations, wear it on.

If your partner knows that you care about her and that she is there to help her with big and small things, they are much more likely to reciprocate. Fulfilling your emotional needs begins with sharing and caring for your partner. A person who feels loved, cared for, and valued is much more likely to reciprocate in kind.

CHAPTER 10:

Society and Culture

The best-case scenario is when all of your friends and the friends of your partner love you as much as they love your mate. It will happen occasionally but rarely is it proper for every friend and every situation. Friends might begin to wonder why your time is being taken up so much with your partner, especially if they are not in a relationship. Friends and Friction

Relationships evolve out of the desire for partners to spend increasing amounts of time around one another, often forgoing anyone else's presence.

It can seem like a shock to friends used to spending all of the time they want at your residence or out doing favorite activities. You suddenly have less time available, which can strike feelings of insecurity, loneliness, or abandonment by close friends.

It's essential to allow them to feel included at times, but you also need to give your partner the healthiest part of your time. If the feelings of resentment and insecurity aren't too drastic, it's a situation that can work when you make the right moves.

Leaving Childhood Friends Behind — Is It necessary

You have to draw a figurative line in the sand for intolerable behaviors. You need to stay in close communication with your partner concerning how friends are treating you and them. You might want to consider a calm confrontation or begin cutting ties if:

- Friends begin to make crude remarks or sexual advances towards your partner.

- Friends are hostile towards you or your partner.

- They bring constant negativity.

- They make increasing demands on your time.

- They tell lies to your partner to try and make them angry towards you.

You might be able to salvage the situation if you have an open and honest discussion with friends about destructive behaviors, but there are times that friendships have to go if you want to stay with your chosen partner.

Eliminating the Third-Wheel Syndrome

Try being more low-key about any plans you have if you find friends suddenly showing up at the same restaurants or events and inviting themselves to hang out. Nothing seems more miserable on a date night than having an unexpected and unwanted third-wheel. You can offer to do a double-date if they want to plan ahead of time, and comfortable for your partner. You will eventually have to begin being somewhat secretive of unique plans with individuals that won't take a subtle hint. Make sure that schedule some time to spend with them on down the line. You don't want your friends to feel you have completely forgotten about them.

Why Can't Everyone Just Get Along?

Personality clashes can also be a huge problem that makes it nearly impossible to be around their friends or have your partner around your friends. It's rarely a group of individuals. You might have one that lets you continuously know how much they can't stand your mate. Unless the friend begins to modify their language and behavior, the friendships tend to fade off. If they genuinely can't stand you or your partner, they will begin to wean themselves away from your presence. It generally is a problem that takes care of itself.

Making Peace with Bffs

Best friends forever. How often have you heard that term? It's worth taking the time to try and work the situation out if it's a friend you or your partner has great affection for and have maintained a long friendship.

Do your best to make your partner's friends feel welcome and included inappropriate events. Avoid rolling your eyes, sighing, or making negative comments when they are around. Remember them on holidays and for their birthday.

Little steps like this can begin to endear you to them, and you'll find their doubts fade away. It eases all manners of insecurity if you keep an open dialogue and demonstrate your care for your partner.

Don't Drag Friends in on Relationship Troubles

Do your level best to not drag friends in on relationship problems. What could be a simple misunderstanding or temporary problem can be blown out of proportion by overly-concerned friends.

It forces them to stick with loyalties and makes it unfair to your partner. It can change the dynamics of their interactions and make everyone feel uncomfortable. You can never be sure if your problems aren't being broadcast across town. Relationship problems are never made better through gossip and conjecture. It can deeply hurt the one you love to hear rumors. If you need to confide in a friend, try and follow these rules:

- Make sure it's a friend you trust.

- Keep it as a generalized question, if possible.

- Never heap all of the blame on your partner.

- Make it understood you are looking for a solution, not to end the relationship.

Reserve Time for Friends and Your Partner

Balancing your free time is the crucial component to making friends and your partner happy. Check ahead with your mate to make sure it's okay to go ahead and make plans to see a movie or head out to a basketball game. Encourage your partner to try and find time to spend with their friends occasionally. Having interests outside the relationship helps keep the growth continuing. To make it possible:

- Make sure your partner has met and is comfortable with the friend you will be hanging out with occasionally.

- Make these outings a reasonable amount and length of time.

- Never cancel plans with your partner to spend time with your friends.

- Give priority days and times to your partner. Maintain the traditions and rituals you've started to create.

Conclusion

You know other married couples. Now, every marriage has its problems. A healthy, conscious couple will still say things they regret to each other. They will have many of the same problems you do.

The difference is that a healthy, conscious couple approaches each disagreement one at a time and comes to a plan of action after a conversation in which both parties feel heard.

To let this happen in your relationship involves setting healthy boundaries and acknowledging and then discussing your differences and disagreements openly. Having a good time together doesn't have to be a chore. It just has to be what you have time to give each other.

Becoming more like this couple is only a matter of emulating this strategy.

So, let's break down all the things this conscious marriage gets right. There are two main parts to this couple's success: problem-solving and communication. Since it always has to come first, we will go into communication first.

You have learned a ton of communication skills and concepts that will help you as you try to express more effectively with your partner. Now, dialectical behavior therapy works the same fundamental way for communication and problem-solving: we deal with one issue at a time.

We don't allow ourselves to do any more than that, because otherwise we will be overwhelmed, and we might as well not communicate at all if we aren't doing it well.

One issue at a time also means each spouse takes turns speaking. When one spouse is talking, the other does not interrupt. All they do is listen. You can nod your head and make eye contact with them to show them that you are really listening to them and not just waiting until your turn to talk.

Before I delve into some other critical points in good communication between a married couple, I would like the two of you to discuss what you think it looks like when a married couple can communicate well. You can think back to a couple of you know who does this effectively, although that might be hard to do because couples don't tend to have these difficult conversations around other people.

Thankfully, you probably have at least some examples of times when the two of you managed to communicate well in a difficult situation. Maybe not everything went perfectly. But you can look back on this example and ask yourselves what went right in that particular instance. You can use it as an example for yourselves for the future so you can communicate more like you did that time.

The other primary way you can practice good communication for a relationship is by using "I" statements and working on all four forms of non-verbal communication: eye contact, body language, emotion, and voice. The more aware you are of all of these, the better you will be at tapping into what makes your spouse tick without upsetting them.

You already have a lot to go off of for what will help you communicate better. As long as you have been doing all the exercises along the way, you are even getting integral practice for improving your relationship communication skills.

Then, there is the other side of what makes a marriage work, and that is problem-solving. You can problem-solve already with your spouse, or else you wouldn't be together right now. However, all of us could improve our problem-solving skills, both inside and outside of our relationships.

As you did for the communication part, I would like to ask both of you to take a moment to discuss what makes for good problem-solving skills. Think back to all the scenarios and ideas we have already gone through to help your thoughts flow. Whatever you come up with, coming up with ideas will be a fruitful way to hone practical communication skills.

The two of you should now think of a time when there was a difficult problem, and you worked it out together. As you have probably realized, problem-solving and communication are positively related things, so they can be hard to separate. But still, you should try to think of a time when the problem was complicated, specifically, not just when you were able to communicate well.

Financial problems can be significant for finding this kind of example. When we go through rough patches with money and have to find places to cut corners, we have to be inventive sometimes and figure out what we will do differently to make sure we are paying our bills.

The answer to problem-solving is always to work through one thing at a time, even when it is tempting to work on many things at once. When confronted with so many problems, we want to force them to work out at once, but life doesn't work that way. Do your best to have just one problem on your mind that you want to work through, and the rest will follow from there.

Another major part of problem-solving is being humble enough to seek out outside help when you need it. If you are too proud to say to an expert, you need help. You are just dragging out your difficulties much longer than they need to drag out.

Men, in particular, tend to have a problem with asking for outside help. They want to have the appearance of always having things all put together, so they can't risk that facade by showing they can't do everything alone by asking for help.

But on the contrary, if you know you are a man who does this, seeking outside help will only make you seem more reasonable. It shows that you care more about figuring out the problem than preserving your pride.

When it comes to problem-solving, you have to know when to keep working through something and walk away. Working hard is a virtue, but hurting yourself by straining yourself on a difficult task isn't always the answer. We can't always solve things with sheer force.

But we can build habits of motivation so that when a seemingly impossible task becomes apparent, we set our sights on something better. I'm not saying we have to be perfect.

Every once in a while, we need to give ourselves a break and approach a new challenge with a positive attitude. Sometimes, our best option is to walk away from it for a while and come back after.

Finally, knowing that what makes marriage work is an effective combination of productive communication and good problem-solving. A couple who has both of these things will still have hard times as everyone does, but the difference is, they will feel equipped to deal with that when it happens. You and your spouse gain the potential to get there if you both put in the work.

Part Four:

Questions for Couples

CHAPTER 1:

Feeling Loved

Knowing your emotional needs and those of your significant other is crucial to your happiness both as individuals and couples.

And because every person has different needs, there is no such thing as a "secret formula for achieving happiness," but rather an ongoing struggle to discover what you subconsciously crave while ensuring that your life partner is also in tune with his or her needs.

According to Dr. Harley, a psychologist and author, the primary emotional needs that people look for in a relationship are affection, admiration, intimate conversation, honesty, sexual fulfillment, physical attractiveness, support (domestic and financial), commitment, and recreational socialization.

Now Dr. Harley points out that each person in the relationship chooses which of these categories and needs apply to them, and more often than not, they end up with different lists.

To dabble a little on the emotional aspect of being in a committed relationship:

1. If you had a magic crystal ball that will tell you the truth about anything (your life, your future, the people in your life), what would you ask it?

2. What one particular thing in your life that you feel grateful for?

3. Which one of us requires more TLC?

4. What movie impressed you the most as a child?

5. What is your biggest fear?

6. Describe the perfect date that we could go on.

7. What do you believe makes people fall in love with each other?

8. What is the best invention that humans have created, up until now, and why? What product/concept/thing would you like to see becoming a reality in the years to come?

9. What do you think about astrology: Is our life course pre-determined by the stars/universe?

10. What is your favorite space in a house, and why?

11. What do you think is the appropriate age for people to get married?

12. What is the weirdest family tradition that your family has? How did it start?

13. What do you think about motivational quotes? Would you use such a quote to decorate a wall in your house? If yes, which one and why?

14. If the apocalypse was coming and you only had 24 hours to prepare yourself, what would you do? Describe your plan in-depth, the items you would gather, the people you'd take with you, and why.

15. Would you say that your personality resembles more of a dog or a cat's personality? What are the characteristics that make you think that?

16. If you had to take away one of your primary senses, which would it be, and how do you think that would alter your life?

17. If we switched lives for a day, what is the thing that you'd most look forward to doing as 'me?'

18. What is the stupidest thing someone ever said to you?

19. What is your go-to comfort food or drink?

20. If you could select a different name for me, what would it be, and why do you think it would suit me?

More Serious Questions

1. How much does love and affection matter to you?

2. What are the four things that we have in common? What about four things that differentiate us?

3. Do you think that we are stronger together? What qualities do we have as a team that we don't individually possess?

4. As a child, how did you show your sadness: throwing tantrums or closing yourself up?

5. If I suddenly got in an accident that left me unable to work, would you be willing to provide for both of us?

6. Do you like that we don't have enough casual conversations? What subjects would you like us to discuss more?

7. Tell me, what are some physical traits I have that made you feel attracted to me?

8. If I chose to modify my body in any shape or form (via plastic surgery), would you support my decision?

9. Tell me what you admire about me, and why.

10. Do you feel like you can depend on me and share your struggles with me, or do you prefer navigating challenging situations alone?

11. In what aspect would you like me to show my affection more/ what am I not doing enough?

12. Would you tell me if you felt embarrassed about something?

13. Are you happy with our sex life, or do you believe it could be better? What should we change/try?

14. What is the greatest and the worst thing about our relationship?

15. Rank the following based on how important are they to you: family, career, love life, self-discovery, and pursuing happiness.

16. Would you prefer that I am always honest with you, even if you might get hurt along the way, or do you think that some things (that have the potential of hurting you) are better left unsaid?

17. If you suddenly get in love with someone else while we are still in a relationship, would you tell me?

18. What does the word 'commitment' mean to you? Do you think you are ready to commit yourself to one person?

19. What was the most crucial lesson that someone ever taught you?

20. What is one thing that you aspire your family knew about you?

21. If you could change any aspect about me, what would it be?

22. Do you get stressed if things don't go according to your ways, or are you okay with ambiguity and not always in control?

23. Do you believe that happiness is something that only people who work hard should achieve and enjoy?

24. How much can someone change, for the sake of their loved one? Name one thing that you could never change about yourself, no matter how hard you tried.

25. Would you define yourself as insecure or confident? Or do you have situations that make you feel insecure, even if you're generally aware of your capabilities and self-worth?

26. In what way does stress affect you? Would you say that you handle stress poorly or effectively?

27. How far on your list of priorities is mental health?

28. Do you believe that it's easier to find happiness when you maintain a positive outlook on life?

29. In your opinion, should your happiness depend on how successful our relationship is, or can a person find happiness on their own?

30. Do you see us getting older together and having our happily ever after? What are the issues that might stand in the way of our happy ending?

Both partners in a relationship should be aware of each other's emotional needs; however, that does not mean that your partner can fulfill every single one of your needs. For example, no matter how strong the bond between you and your significant other is, they can never solve all your insecurities. Self-love, self-esteem, self-worth, and confidence are things that you need to nurture and find within yourself. If you have a distorted self-image, no number of compliments from your partner will help you see yourself through their eyes, and it's unfair to expect them to fix your issues.

CHAPTER 2:

Personal Boundaries

What Should I Never Say to You in Anger or Playfulness?

There are certain words or phrases in your head that reach the line for suitable vocabulary.

Everyone has their understanding of what the threshold is. There may be playful name-calling that is all right, but other names that are profoundly hurting. You could find some words that are so nasty and demeaning that you don't want to hear them, even in jest — but particularly in anger.

Have You shared all Your Boundaries with Me? If Not, what Are They?

If you appear to be the right person, you could encourage your partner to cross your borders unknowingly. For your partner to live up to your limits, you must be mindful of yourself and interact entirely and freely.

Find out from each other what personal boundaries are essential to each of you.

Is There Anything I Do Now that Crosses Your Boundaries and Makes You uncomfortable?

If you're not conscious of your limits, you may not be able to answer this question without some consideration. We often have a vague feeling of unease or frustration in our relationship, but we're unsure why we feel that way. It's also because our partner is doing something to cross a personal boundary. This can include, for example, sex, disruption of time, preferences, or privacy needs.

In what Ways Do You View Me as a unique individual, Separate and apart from Our Relationship?

Before you were a couple, each of you had a sense of self and personal identity. You've built a unified identity as a pair, but that doesn't mean you can lose your individuality. Each partner should respect and appreciate the other as a single person, not merely as an extension of the relationship.

Do You Feel free to Be Yourself and Express Yourself with Me? If Not, Why?

We can lose part of our identity when we enter into an intimate relationship. Often this happens when we're looking at the other individual to help us define ourselves. It can also occur when one spouse is more dominant, and the other accommodates or approves to preserve peace.

If you're not free or willing to be yourself and express yourself, not only do you sacrifice your self-esteem, but you also deprive your partner of the ability to know you fully and completely.

Is There Anything about Our Sexual Relationship that Makes You unlucky or uncomfortable? If So, Then what?

It can be difficult to openly discuss differences in sexual desires or needs, especially if you aren't comfortable with something your partner is doing or saying during sex or have differing sex drives. If you aren't compatible sexually, it can undermine intimacy in your relationship, primarily if you don't address it. By discussing your sexual desires and wishes, you both can find a middle ground that feels acceptable and comfortable. Each of you might need to compromise at times to meet the needs of the other.

Are There any physical Belongings or Spaces in Our Home that You Would Like to Have as Your Own?

Couples frequently establish a pattern of "What's yours is mine, and what's mine is yours." If you live together, you'll share several belongings and physical spaces in your home. However, you may have belongings that you don't want to release as a "couple thing." Maybe it's your laptop or your favorite coffee mug. You do not want to share your razor or give up your pillow. This need will apply to the spaces in your home. One or both of you might need a personal "sanctuary" of your own.

Do You Ever Feel Awkward Saying "No" Or Thinking for Yourself with Me? If So, Then Why?

Healthy self-esteem requires we feel confident speaking up for ourselves, even if it feels uncomfortable or creates conflict. There are occasions to keep the peace, but if it becomes your fallback place, you're creating an unhealthful disparity in your relationship. You diminish your partner's regard for you, and you lower your self-esteem. If you're the spouse who always seems to get his or her way, you're equally responsible for managing by getting to the root of the matter. Find out why your loved one doesn't tell what they're talking about, and explore how you can both fix the issue.

Where Are You Not Able to Compromise?

But as unique people, you have beliefs, ambitions, and expectations that you can't compromise. One of you might feel strongly about his or her religion, but the other does not hold the same values. You may be a committed vegetarian, but your partner isn't ready to give up consuming meat. You should all have principles and ideals.

How Are We Going to Approach It if a Boundary Has Been Crossed?

Knowledge of each other's expectations goes a long way towards creating a friendly and loving environment where you both want to meet each other's needs. However, you will inevitably cross each other's boundaries from time to time. We are imperfect and forgetful and can get caught up in our own needs. To minimize potential conflict over boundary issues, create a proactive plan for handling it when one of you steps over the comfort line with the other. Humor goes a long way in deflecting irritation and defensiveness. Perhaps you can create a funny line or cue to remind each other of your boundaries gently.

CHAPTER 3:

Sex and Affection

Issues concerning sexual intimacy are just the tip of the iceberg when it comes to healthy relationships. In other words, they are typically indications of a broader-rooted emotional disorder under the surface.

Physical and emotional problems frequently go hand in hand, from less snuggling, touching, and kissing to less frequent (or inexistent) sex. And of course, barring medical conditions, the prevalence of physical contact is also related to the relationship's wellbeing. "I also see a symbiotic relationship between enjoyment, emotional intimacy, and the fulfillment of relationships, each one of these interacts with the other to affect our appetite and excitement. The growing couple is unique, and some people are keener on physical contact than others. But if you start feeling a widening distance between you and your partner.

Questions for Couple

- What if we are not very comfortable talking about our sex life in sessions?
- How often do you want sex?
- How do we improve our sex life?

- How can we be more aware of areas where our habits are incompatible?
- Are you happy with my self-care and hygiene?
- What sexual desires can we enjoy with each other?

Typical Issues Related to Sex and Affection

Dissimilar Libido

This is when one partner is more willing to want sex than the other, remarkably regular. It can lead to anything, from slight frustration to deep anger and hatred feelings.

Our emotional Connection Is lacking

Although it's Cool if both persons are in it only for the physical release, if you want an intimate relationship but don't feel it, things become more brackish. That is also called as "empty sex," which doesn't sound particularly attractive. To help banish the feeling, work outside of the bedroom to encourage intimacy. "Spend more time together, find new, popular experiences that can help you build a connection, and discuss in other ways what brings joy to you and your partner.

Some Couples Just Don't Have enough Sex or regular Sex Life

Once the honeymoon period has off, this one also forces its way into relationships. Fortunately, compromises will save the day. "Discuss how much you'd like to be sexually involved, then hammer out a schedule in the middle ground, or set a date you've already decided to be active and have a regular list of things you'd like to do, which could be an issue as well.

Loss of or Lack of physical Intimacy

More often than not, the loss or lack of physical intimacy begins in the head. Physical or emotional isolation is often a coping mechanism that evolved years earlier. The problem is, it can fester distrust and exacerbate the divide in the relationship.

There is also an explanation of why men and women's withdrawal will vary, so it's necessary to consider both sides of the coin. For an individual, the physical is generally connected directly to his ego. When this aspect of a relationship is in trouble, the emotional bond inside the relationship diminishes. On the other hand, women seek an emotional connection more often, and they will physically withdraw without it. In general, a woman must first wind out of the bedroom, speak, and communicate emotionally.

Different Sexual Styles & Lack of Communication

Love is blind, and to bring something different to the table (or bed) for each partner is essential. But such differences may also result in a lack of interactions among the couples. Some of the most common problems include starting couples not being on the same side. These can involve libido variations, impulses, dreams, and challenges of excitement. "Still, people find it difficult to express their desires and have open dialogues about enjoyment and sexual contact.

Infidelity

Nothing can break a friendship like an indiscretion. They are acting with couples with over three decades of experience.

Men are much visual and rate their sex life as an enormous way to connect with their partners. When that's absent or rare in a relationship, issues of desire, competence, and interest arise. These issues can take a man to 'test' his level of attraction with other women, whether at work or as stupid as somewhere like a grocery store or a local shop."

CHAPTER 4:

Personal Habits

Are Your personal and Home Hygienic Standards compatible?

This is a more critical area, then many people realize. People often feel there are a right way and a wrong way to maintain household order and cleanliness. It usually depends on what you picked up from childhood. Their method is, of course, the right way, and anything else is wrong. For example, if you like your home to have a casual, comfortable, lived-in look, you may tend to perceive someone neat and orderly as fastidious and "uptight." However, if you like it clean and tidy, you will likely be offended by what you perceive as the sloppiness of your casual partner.

Many engaged couples feel they can quickly train their partners to conform to "the correct way" after marriage. They believe that once their partners see "how much better the correct way is, they will change." Unfortunately, this is not true, and fights about this issue can polarize an otherwise happy couple. Moreover, sadly, the more they fight, the more dissimilar they become. This because we tend to become more focused and even more entrenched on issues, we feel strongly about each time our "stubborn" partners refuse to understand our point of view. In time, couples start to think there is something wrong with the other's mind.

"He's a neurotic germ probe," I sometimes hear, or "she's a hoarder," or "a control freak."

Can You Change these Differences After Marriage?

Yes. But not easily; and, sadly, not always. However, before marriage, we have choices, but this is where we can easily fool ourselves.

Interestingly, one way to resolve this difficulty is for each person to accept the other's way as valid for that person. In other words, the other person does not insist that the casual person also be neat, nor does the casual one requires a more relaxed attitude on the part of their "fastidious" mate. In other words, you grant your partner the right to be or do things his or her way. To accomplish this, you will have to see the issue from a different perspective, i.e., your partner has as much right to their course as you have to yours. Thus, you would see the issue more like your problem and less as a nuisance caused by your partner. Therefore, if you like it neat, you make it that way and not insist that your partner frequently tidy up. In time, paradoxically, there is a tendency for loving couples to see some value in their partner's way and move closer together.

Nevertheless, I taught Personal Psychology or Human Relations in college for several years. I found my classes of around fifty mixed young and older adults divided, often sharply, on this issue. A good percentage felt so strongly about their position they were not open to debate.

Be warned. It isn't easy to be comfortable living with poles apart from you in this area. Complaints about neatness and cleanliness are among the more frequent and destructive in marriage. Consider this area carefully.

It is important to note that our household standard usually reflects more than just fastidiousness or sloppiness about the house. This issue points to an overall behavioral style. Personality dimensions fall on continuums, and the one-dimension spectrum is from obsessive/compulsive at one extreme to impulsive on the other.

Obsessive/compulsive people manifest an over preoccupation with orderliness, perfectionism, and control.

They are often rigid and inflexible.

Impulsive people are just the opposite.

They are usually careless in their manner and put little thought into their decisions. The potential for incompatibility here is glaring with a high likelihood of severe clashes involving the home and everyday life.

CHAPTER 5:

Disagreements and Differences

How Should We Handle any Conflicts and Disagreements?

There will be many conflicts that occur in your connection, especially if the two of you are together for a very long time. It is essential to know how each of you will handle conflicts to work together and get the best results in the process.

Dealing with conflicts in the wrong manner is not going to do the relationship any favors at all. It is essential to get you both on the same page. If one of you goes into a rage at a disagreement, one works with the silent treatment so that nothing gets solved, or one runs away. This will not help add more strength to the relationship.

Some of the best ways that you can work on these disagreements (and there are going to be plenty of them over the term of your relationship) includes:

An Environment that Allows for Open Communication

In any healthy relationship, both of you need to communicate in an open matter about what is bothering you and what you feel like is going well. You need to not only spend your time talking about things when problems arise in the relationship. This can get boring and can shut down communication as you both get tired of just being negative together all the time. This makes the conversation more comfortable to handle and ensures that no one in the relationship feels like everything they are doing is wrong.

Suppose you or your partner feel like you cannot talk openly about important things to you and the relationship, such as aspirations, money, and life issues.

Try to Be respectful, Even When Things Get heated

There are going to be times when your conversations and your conflicts can get a bit heated. But, despite this, you need to work on maintaining a demeanor that is respectful and calm throughout it all. Don't cross the line at any point and start throwing insults at your partner. You need to ensure that the focus stays on the current conflict and don't try to pull your partner down or do personal jibes to them. No matter the leading cause of this argument, no one should make you feel uncomfortable or yell at you during this time. This is not a time for anyone to attack and yell at each other. It is time to work together to come up with a solution that works.

Get to the Root of this Problem

Sometimes when you start arguing with your partner, your needs or your partner's needs are not met. Is it possible that all of these little issues that your partner is bringing up could be related to a more significant problem?

For example, if you find that your partner is upset that you are gone in the middle of the week with your friends rather than home with them, they may be upset that you are not designating more time for the relationship. Or maybe it stresses them out about you keeping your grades up during this time of year so that you can get to your goals. Consider things from your partner and consider how you would feel if the roles were reversed. This can help you figure out the root of the problem and make it easier to find a solution, rather than making them feel bad because their concern seems small.

Be careful about the Arguments that Are more about Control

If you feel like your partner is fighting with you because they want to control what you do, this should be a big red flag against them, and you may need to get some help. If your partner is mad at some silly things like you texting people of the opposite sex, doesn't like how you prioritize school and other responsibilities over them, or pressures you to hook up with them while limiting the time that you get to spend with others, then these are signs that your partner is trying to control you.

Find some Ground that You Both Can Agree to

As a couple, you likely want to work together to get through any problems that arise and ensure that you feel respected and love. And the best way that you can do this is to learn how to find some middle ground. Finding a balance between what both you and your partner want and what you can both be comfortable with can be crucial to avoid too much conflict and make your relationship much happier.

Suppose you both genuinely care about the relationship and making it work. In that case, you will learn how to agree on things that cause these conflicts, without feeling like you, or them, have to make significant sacrifices to maintain the relationship. Compromising will be crucial because it will help you resolve your conflicts, no matter what they are, and find the middle ground. However, it seems hard at the moment; it can be a lot easier than you think.

Learn how to Choose Your Battles

Do you need to waste your valuable time and effort, and cause a rift in a relationship, because there are a few socks on the floor? If the problem is small, it is sometimes better to drop it all and enjoy your night more than just pushing it and getting into a big fight.

If you look at the problem and realize that you will not be that mad about it in a week, it is probably not worth your energy. With most of the issues that the two of you will fight over, it is not worth your time or effort.

Consider whether the Issue Is Something that You Can Resolve or Not

Sometimes we end up arguing with our partner, and it is about something big, something that will impact our lives. These can sometimes cause some conflicts if you find out that the two of you have different goals here, and it can go into disagreement as you try to figure out the middle ground.

CHAPTER 6:

Time Together and alone

What Exactly Is Our Goal?

Generally, the purpose of a relationship is finding someone you can dwell with, someone who understands you and accepts you despite all the flaws they can see.

It is about finding love, joy, happiness in the arms of someone, proceeding further to make a family together.

It is okay to start, not knowing what you want.

But further down the line, your ignorance becomes dangerous for you and your partner.

Relationships need a solid foundation to stand on.

And that foundation consists of the goals you and your partner have built.

Would it not be sad if your relationship had nothing else to stand on?

Here are some goals that can be implemented into your relationship, even your marriage, for a happier and more prosperous future:

- **To Remain Best Friends Forever**

  While you and your partner were dating, if you are now married, you were just friends. Their schedules get in the way, and life becomes too full of time activities and even fights chip in to take a piece out of the friendship. Before you realize it, you will find yourself having dinner with a stranger.

- **More Time Together and Fun**

  Earlier on in the relationship, there were a lot of dates, meetups, and hangouts. You both spent a lot of time basking in the comfort of each other's presence. That was a priority. Do not let it fade away from your relationship.

- **Make It a Priority to Spend some alone Time with one Another and Have Fun Together each Week.**

  You could take a walk, stay in and eat or watch a movie, or whatever causal plans you might want to implement. Keep it simple, fun, and argument free.

- **Work as a Team**

  As a couple, you have to stop being a 'me and you' thing and become a 'we,' or an 'us.'

  Whatever you might face should meet you both together, working as a team. Whatever issues might arise, it is not a problem for one of you to face, but a wall that must be tackled together.

- **Keep the Channels of Communication Open**

  A lot of barriers occur in a relationship due to a lack of proper communication. And thus, unspoken needs, expectations, and wants arise. Assumptions occur, and in the end, all it brings is frustration. Make it a priority always to maintain an open channel of communication with one another.

- **Consistently Appreciate each other**

  Daily appreciation of your partner should be a priority. It could be through means as simple as a "thank you," a "good job," or a surprise note, telling your spouse that you see them, acknowledge them, and appreciate them.

  Notice nothing but the good things they do and continuously show your appreciation for that.

- **Give Everything to the Relationship and Then some more**

A lot of couples share the responsibility of managing the relationship equally. You give half and expect your partner to produce the rest. This is troublesome because it could lead to:

a. Pointless

b. Scorekeeping,

c. Bitterness,

d. Resentment and arguments.

Important issues could arise about either one of you being maltreated. Still, you cannot talk about it because you have been so focused on making sure each person does a certain amount, so the situation would be hard to confront.

Learn to give all that you have into your relationship, focusing on that and not what you get in return.

- **Never Threaten Your Partner**

Always view your commitment seriously.

When you threaten the relationship, you are only causing harm. Make it your goal never to threaten the relationship or your dedication to it in an argument.

- **Keep Your Attention on each other's Strengths**

  Both of you are strong and weak in different aspects. More often than we realize, it is easy to focus on the imperfections, rather than the parts that make us useful.

- **Always Be There for one Another**

  One of the most reassuring moments of life is knowing that you have your back, someone who will console you and lift your spirits whenever you feel low.

  Become that person to your partner. Always be there for them through the pains of life and the sunny moments after the storm.

- **Do Your best to Handle Issues and Disagreements Intelligently**

  Make it a mission always to fix your squabbles wisely, respectfully, and together as a team. At the first sign of the trouble growing, take a step back and stop yourselves from hurting each other. Doing this will ensure that no situation gets the best of you.

- **Be the expert You Can Be for Your Partner**

  In whatever you do that involves your partner, always put your best foot forward.

Do you have a date coming up? Dress up in your cutest outfit and look your best for them.

Are you making dinner? Pull out everything the stops and make it look like it's from a five-star restaurant. Treat your partner like royalty.

- **Relentlessly Support each other's Dreams and Goals**

  You both have dreams and goals. Just because it is not yours does not mean you cannot be supportive. Remember that in a relationship, both of you are a team. Be each other's wingmen and push one another in the direction of the goal.

- **Always Forgive**

  We are not impervious to mistakes.

  Occasionally, we all mess up. If a list of all our mistakes were put together, it would be quite a sight. Be quick to forgive and let go.

  Choosing not to forgive not only harms you but your relationship as well. So, let go of that offense that hurt you and move on.

- **View Your Relationship in the long-Term**

  Speak and talk as if you will be together for a very long time and mean it. Plan and dream with each other. Outline what you would like to see and happen years down the road.

- **Discuss Your Dreams with the One You Love**

  You should be able to deliver your hopes and aspirations with your partner. It should be easy letting them know the plans you made as a kid — even the ones you saw as silly or childish. Your partner is your support system.

CHAPTER 7:

Spiritual Life and Values

T his can be hard when individuals are brought into the same relationship, and they come with different thoughts and backgrounds.

Some of the Best Questions to Help Spouses Connect More Include:

- **How Do We Handle When Things Get tough?**

  Things are not consistent with being as perfect as you would like. And that is fine. But you have to realize that you need to be there for one another. There are times when you will fight, and you won't see eye to eye, but this doesn't mean that you get to be difficult, that you get to be mean or cruel, or that you get to forget why you got married to your spouse in the first place.

- **Are There any Reasons that We Would both (or one or the Other) Consider Divorce?**

  This one can be a tough one for many couples. They often don't want to admit that things would cause them to leave the marriage. Or maybe they don't want to ever think about the marriage ending, so they don't want to focus on this question at all. And then there are times when one spouse hasn't thought about divorce or the conditions that would make them leave, and the other partner has thought about it; this one can escape the former feeling like they are being punched in the stomach.

  But for this question, you need to get this out in the open. This isn't to cause hurt feelings or to make the couple uncomfortable. But it is there to ensure that you have open communication and talk about this ahead of time.

- **What Can My Spouse Do for Me to Add more Intimacy into Our Lives?**

Intimacy, whether sexual or other forms, is essential in a marriage. While most partners will usually agree that they enjoy this intimacy, and this time they get to spend together in a marriage, it is unfortunate that this marital intimacy is often pushed to the side.

This can cause several issues in the marriage. To start with, if one spouse or the other is the only one pushing it aside, it will leave the other one out in the cold. The spouse may feel that you no longer love them and harbor resentment against you for not wanting to show this intimacy. And this is often a big reason why one spouse will start to look outside the marriage to find this intimacy.

Make a promise to never use familiarity as a weapon, tool, or a way to manipulate the other partner. God's design for marriage was to include this intimacy. Therefore, it is not a part of God's plan to hold off with intimacy with our partner, outside of predetermined (and agreed upon) reasons in the marriage, such as after a child's birth.

- **What Are Five Things that You Find as special about Your Spouse?**

One of the best things that you can do for your spouse is to let them know how special they are to you.

Maybe you like their smile, how they work well with the kids, how hard they work, how they try to make things easier when you come home, their laugh, their sense of adventure, and more. Don't just go through this list, though. Spend some of your focus on your spouse, and decide which characteristics and attributes are essential to you, and the ones that you appreciate about your spouse in specific.

- **Are There any Things that You Would Like to Fix?**

  There will be some things that you like about your spouse in any marriage, and then there are those things that you would like your spouse to work on to fix. This doesn't mean that you get to come into the conversation and be mean to them all of the time.

  Both you and your spouse can join together to work on this part. Sit down, and each takes a turn writing out some of the things that you would like to see improved in the relationship. You can discuss what you think the spouse needs to improve on, what you would like to see improved about the marriage, and more.

- **Do You Think There Are any Other Ways that You Can Invite God into Your Marriage?**

  You and your spouse need to focus on in your marriage to invite God into it. Even Christian couples will forget to do this often, which will add to the troubles. The world is complicated enough, and everywhere we look, we can see that some things are going on that we should not be a part of. But if you don't invite God into your marriage, and make Him the foundation of a healthy marriage, then it is going to be easy for you to give into some of the temptations that our world has to offer.

- **Should My Spouse and I Start Praying Together?**

There is nothing more powerful than praying with your spouse. This is a very spiritual time, one where both of you can speak up to the desires that are on your heart, where you can connect on a deeper level than before, and where you will be able to both ask God for some help in a situation that you are going through.

Maybe take five minutes before going to bed to pray together, whether it is just talking to God about your day and the things that you would like to see improved, or if you would like to say an Our Father or Hail Mary together. The choice is up to you, as long as you can spend some time together praying to God.

CHAPTER 8: **Work**

What Is Your Dream Job?

The way you discuss this will depend on where you are in your life, your age, and where you are in the relationship. You can also split this into two things. The first one is their actual dream job and what they would like to set their goals and aims towards. The second is a make-believe job, just for fun, that they would do if they could.

You can then take the time afterward to discuss both of the dream jobs and how you can work together to make sure that both of you can get there.

Maybe you find that there is a way that these dream jobs can go together, but your plan may have to be a bit different. You may not be able to support one of you working to be a doctor while the other open their own business because this takes a lot of money, time, and dedication. But maybe one of you will work towards their goals for a bit, and then when those are met, you can let the other one.

There are some cases where both of you will be able to reach your goals simultaneously. Two people are working on their purposes all by themselves, without any of the support from the other, wastes a lot of time and energy. But when they work together on their goals and are on the same team, it becomes much more comfortable.

This is an excellent time for both of you to stop and figure out what you would like to do in the future. To consider with this, include:

First, consider some of your skills. These skills can be useful when looking for a job that would work the best for you and make you feel satisfied with your work.

Think about the things that you aim you could be doing daily. Have you ever worked on a hobby and hoped that someone would pay you to keep doing this? Even if you can find something that you would enjoy doing from one day to another, rather than feeling like you were going to dread going to work each day.

You need to figure out your passion. A dream job is not one you show up to from one day to another because you have to. A dream job is something that you will enjoy doing, something that looks at your passions and allows you to have some fun. Think about some of the desires you have, some of the things you enjoy doing, and then let this be your guide to finding the perfect dream job.

Another thing to consider is saying to your partner about this. Ask them what they think your dream job may be. There might be some silly things that come out as you both joke about the dream jobs of one another. But there could also be some places where they bring up topics and ideas that you might not have considered in the past. Your partner often will see some things about you that even you had missed out on in the past. Asking them for some guidance and asking why they would suggest one job over another can give you a more in-depth insight into your own life and some of the things you might enjoy doing.

As you think about some of the things you would enjoy doing in a job, take some time to talk about this with your partner. Explore what would make you happy, whether the dream job is possible (don't use this as a way to put them down, but be realistic about what can happen).

CHAPTER 9:

Goals and Dreams

You'll want to focus on answering the first set of questions for yourself, honoring your truth, before tackling any further questions as a couple.

You may also find that you're reluctant to share these answers with your partner right away; that's perfectly fine. You can decide to keep all these replies to yourself or pick and choose which parts to share.

The purpose of these questions is to refocus on managing your expectations for the future. This exercise is not designed to grade your competence or compatibility.

Pose this Set of Questions to Yourself:

- Do you have specific or detailed plans for the following year?
- After five years?
- After a decade?
- Any plans that stretch even further into the future than a decade?
- Do you find you tend to think more in the long term or short term?

- Would you instead daydream about what you'll do this weekend, what you'll do following summer, or what you'll do five years from now?
- What do you imagine your soon major purchase or financial investment will be? (Define the term "major" on a sliding scale here; either something worth a full month's salary or more or a larger purchase than you've made since you entered this relationship.)
- Do you feel that you're done with education? Or would you like to pursue it further?
- Do you have further ambitions for your career?
- If so, how close are you to realizing them?
- When it's time to settle down long-term, do you know where you'd like to live?
- Do you feel well-equipped to become a parent?
- Is there a specific age or deadline by which you expect to reach particular goals? (For example, you might plan to have your own business before you start a family or to retire by the time your child graduates from college.)
- When you look forward to the future, are there any significant circumstances in your life that you know will need to change to reach your goals? If so, what are they?
- Do you have a plan to change these circumstances?
- If so, do you think you'd be comfortable discussing these anxieties with your partner or someone else in your support system?
- Do you consider these fears and anxieties to be rational, irrational, or somewhere in between?

- Do you feel like you've changed or grown a lot within the past year?
- If so, how? And are you happy with the change?
- How do you think you might grow or change within five years?
- How do you feel about getting older? Do you look forward to it, or does the thought of aging cause your anxiety?
- What is one thing that you are worried you might not accomplish before your age disables you?

It's crucial to feel reliable about your future desires before you make any attempt to tailor them for your partner's sake.

Where Are We headed as a Couple?

This following set of questions concerns your future trajectory as a pair.

Don't feel any pressure to get through all these questions in one session or even all in one week. Your collective future deserves deep thought and consideration. If any of these questions expose a disparity, in terms of what you're each expecting from your future together, take some time to discuss the issue. How important is this goal to each of you, and how flexible can you be? Is this an instance wherein you might work together to design a compromise? Or could you each pursue your own separate goals without pulling too much energy or attention away from the relationship?

There are no road maps or blueprints to adhere to; prescribed gender roles and notions of what a typical couple should look like and how it should operate are changing every day. Don't be afraid to make outlandish suggestions for compromise, or to negotiate powerfully for your own needs in the relationship. Rather than worrying over how your relationship should progress, focus instead on how it does work now, and how it can work even better in the future to serve you both.

- In what ways do you worry that our goals won't align in the years ahead?
- How do you feel about our current divisions of responsibility?
- Do you see any need for our respective roles in this relationship to change or evolve in the future?
- When you envision the future, how much time do you think we'd spend together over a typical week?
- Do you know whether or not you'd like to be a primary caregiver to pets or children in the future?
- If you're not yet certain, are you comfortable discussing your hesitations and concerns with me?

(Keep this discussion vague and hypothetical, or skip it entirely for now, if the subject is especially sensitive for you.)

- Do you think we've grown or changed as a couple over the past year?
- If so, how? And are you happy with the change?
- How much do you expect our relationship to grow or change in the coming year?
- How do you expect to handle unforeseen challenges to our plans?

- Can you list three goals that you're excited for us to pursue together in the future? Think long term here.
- Can you list three challenges you expect us to face in the future that worry you?
- Finally, can you suggest three (or more) strategies to overcome those challenges as a team?
- This is an excellent point to take a little break and check-in with yourself. How do you feel about these answers? Did you notice any similarities in your future personal plans and your collective plans? Or did you find that your partner's following few steps are heading in a different direction than you expected?
- If your goals are already quite similar, you might want to talk instead about how your relationship will fare if these goals suddenly become unreachable--for instance, if a large percentage of your focus is on building a family together, how might your relationship handle a struggle with infertility or inability to adopt?

Furthermore, if your goals are already aligned, you will need to make a concerted effort to hold onto your own identities within the relationship. Still, in reality, these are not healthy ideals to strive for. It's reasonable to perform selfless acts from time to time and make small personal sacrifices to build something great together. Still, without healthy boundaries, you could easily give too much of yourself to your relationship and wind up feeling drained or neglected.

Conclusion

Ask yourself, "What else do I want to know about you? About our relationship?" Then tune in to your own body and wait. Imagine you're tuning in to a radio signal that includes feelings, mental images, and physical sensations. Notice what arises within — physically, energetically, emotionally, or in the form of visual images — in response to the question you've asked (this is an abbreviated version of "Focusing," a powerful self-awareness technique created by Eugene Gendlin). Once you've gotten clarity on what this "what else" might be for you, it's time to begin creating a round of unique, quiz-style questions of your own.

Step 1. Write down your open-ended, multiple-choice, or true/false questions.

Step 2. Vet your questions for barbs or hidden motives. You'll connect most successfully with your partner when your questions are free of agendas and projections.

For example, if your question is "What was the name of the best lover you've ever had?" get clear on why you want to know this. If your partner gives you an answer you don't want to hear, will it distance you? If a question is emerging from your anxiety, try changing it to something that will help you learn more about your partner no matter what they respond.

Step 3. Prepare yourself to release any attachment to your partner's answer. Monitor your feelings and judgments once they respond. Whatever questions you ask in a committed love relationship, the key to creating a fruitful exchange is being mindful of (and responsible for) your feelings, needs, and fears.

Step 4. Practice listening in a way that implicitly communicates approval and acceptance.

Develop a back-and-forth listener-speaker style of communication in which both partners equitably share roles and "air time." Structuring communication can help you both listen and speak productively. This may mean getting yourself into the right headspace before asking questions. By reminding yourself that your partner is a separate person, entitled to their thoughts, dreams, feelings, preferences, and past experiences, you're creating a safe, neutral zone where they can share themselves more honestly and authentically with you. Setting the intention to listen with love and be mindful of your hidden motives goes a long way toward helping your partner share who they indeed are.

Step 5. Check-in with your partner to see if they're emotionally available before blurting out your questions. You may want to come up with a specific time of the day and the week that's your designated "Question Time," so you're both prepared and in the right mindset to quiz each other and create your own personal Quiz Master Challenges.

Step 6. When your partner asks you a question, do your best to answer it honestly, sincerely, and with an open heart. If you're the questioner, avoid judging your partner's responses. Let the meaning and implications of their answers sink in. Be sure to thank each other for asking questions and after answering, too. Your curiosity about one another is a gift — a sign that you care about. Your willingness to share and disclose is also a gift — an act of trust.

Part Five:

How to Overcome Depression

CHAPTER 1:

What Is Depression and How to Recognize It?

How Is Anxiety developed?

We all have fears. Some are afraid of the dark (no shame in it!), some people are afraid of more abstract things like changing and trying out new things, some people are afraid of public speaking – whichever the fear and whatever the reason, the bottom line is that feeling fear is normal. Fear is a natural response our mind has to help us survive, which means that being afraid may make you cautious of some things that may pose a threat to your well-being. If you see a man in a hood stalking from an alley in the middle of the night, you are more likely to feel fear, which is a good thing since you are being alarmed by your mind that something is wrong, which further causes a response set to protect you from harm. However, feeling anxious and having an anxiety disorder will prevent you from truly living and enjoying life.

We now know how fear is formed and why, but how is anxiety formed and developed and why some fears transform into an anxiety disorder?

Anxiety is a severe problem, especially when allowed to develop freely, usually when a person affected by this disorder feeds their fears and doubts. Anxiety may cause physical weakness, heart palpitations, and tremors, difficulties with breathing, nausea, and even seizures in more progressive anxiety disorder cases. But how is anxiety developed?

It takes years for anxiety to develop fully. Simultaneously, in this process, each negative experience builds one upon another until the feeling of anxiety becomes entirely debilitating for the person suffering from this disorder. Even though it may sound simple, anxiety is formed by combining different factors, where your brain creates past and present experiences, traumas, personality, and hormones. Scientists also believe that anxiety and many different mental disorders may run in the family, so genetics is one of the recurring factors. Beyond genetics, a person may develop anxiety disorder when frequently or periodically faced stressful situations that cause a natural defensive response in our brain, known as "flight or fight." Our body is a complex mechanism designed to protect us and keep us going. One of these complex mechanisms is the "flight or fight" mode, triggered whenever a stressful or dangerous situation appears. Some common signs of anxiety disorders are extremely stressful situations such as being in a toxic relationship, working on a job position that you don't enjoy and finding stressful, continuous stress, feeding your fears, and inability to recognize situations non-harmful. Anxiety is usually developed in early adulthood and childhood, which means that the way you are raised may also create anxiety disorder and traumatic experiences you have gone through in your life. Abuse and neglect are some of the common factors for developing anxiety in early childhood. At the same time, finances and unhappy love life are the most common stress-inducing factors that feed anxiety and further develop. The bottom line is different factors may cause anxiety to develop over time. Still, regardless of the reason, the most important fact to note is that anxiety IS treatable with CBT and DBT techniques proven to be some of the most effective treatments in anxiety disorder.

Another essential thing to note is that every person is faced with everyday anxieties. We all have worries and fears. Still, if anxiety is prolonged to the point where fearing and worrying becomes a regular part of your life, you need to seek help and resolve your mental condition to live a happy life.

How Is Depression Developed?

A significant number of factors are noted by psychologists and doctors in connection to developing depression. While numerous different factors can affect a person towards developing depressive disorders, one thing is sure and in common to all cases of depression – just like it is the case with anxiety, depression is developing over a more extended time and is a result of more than several negative experiences and factors that are defined as triggers.

In some cases, depression is diagnosed due to chemical imbalance. However, the development of depressive disorder is far more complicated and convoluted. Life events may trigger depression and feed already present risk factors. In contrast, a single event may cause depression to appear if a patient has already had impending depression symptoms. In most cases, a series of negative experiences and traumas need to take place over a more extended time to get depression. Frequent exposure to stress and stressful situations and events like losing your job or experiences, such as being in a toxic relationship, may affect the patient to develop depressive disorders. Stress is most certainly one of the primary triggers of depression. While all people in the world are going to stressful situations, not everyone develops depression as a result, which means that risk factors need to be present to cause depressive disorder symptoms. Often, patients suffer from a chemical imbalance, specifically related to the brain's part designed to regulate mood. Another risk factor and a probable cause of depression, combined with a chemical imbalance and external factor, is genetics. Specific genes prove that depression can be inherited through DNA if there is a history of mental illness running in the family.

Besides changes in the brain and how your brain releases essential chemicals combined with other risk factors such as genetics and stressful life events and experiences, depression is more likely to develop due to certain personal features that a person might have. Personality also plays a significant role in developing a depressive disorder, so in case you have low self-esteem, you tend to worry a lot about everything and anything. If you are inclined to criticize yourself and develop negative case scenarios in your mind, you are more likely to become depressed and develop a depressive disorder.

CHAPTER 2:

Positive Psychology

Harnessing the Power of Positivity

One of the first elements that helped me significantly in overcoming anxiety in love is the power of positive thinking.

"Is your glass half-empty or half-full?" What is your answer to this question? How you answer this timeless question gauges your outlook on life. Do you focus more on the empty part of the glass or the filled part of the glass? Do you have an optimistic or pessimistic approach?

Positivity attracts positivity, which means to say the more you build your positivity, the more it will be cover all aspects of your life. Referred to as the law of attraction, this concept is based on the idea that what you desire and live by will attract more of the same thing.

If you are anxious, cynical, and insecure, you are likely to attract negativity, and the reverse is also true. Which means to say if you are filled with negativity, you will attract anxiety, cynicism, insecurity, and other harmful things into your life.

A classic example is the legendary story of Walt Disney. Did you know that the top US newspaper editor fired him before becoming famous because he was not creative enough? If he had believed in this negative feedback, the world would have lost the magic of Disney.

Instead of being bogged down by negativity, Walt Disney believed he had what he takes for success and simply persisted in his efforts. The universe gave him his desire. That is the power of positive thinking.

What is positive thinking? The mental and emotional attitude focuses on the right and positive aspects that benefit the thinker. Positive thinking drives you to anticipate good health, success, happiness, and joy and drive you to achieve these elements through persistent hard work.

Despite all the benefits of positive thinking, the human mind seems to be designed for negativity. We seem to be predisposed to negative things. We tend to focus more on dark emotions, including sadness, depression, anger, pain, insecurity, disappointment, etc. than on happy emotions like gratitude, contentment, joy, etc. Even when we reflect on our lives, we tend to focus on things that gave pain and forget about things that gave us joy and happiness.

Give yourself a test. Before leaving for work, look at two pictures: a cute little puppy and another that depicts a violent crime. As the day progresses, you will see that you are likely to forget the cute little puppy's picture and recall the violent crime picture often. And this is when you are consciously doing this activity.

Unconsciously, you might not recall the picture of the puppy even once during the day. But the other one will remain in your mind for a long time. You might even discuss it with your colleagues. It is more or less natural for the human mind to skew towards negativity. However, it is possible to shift this attitude and get your mind to think positive thoughts. And there is a science behind this behavior defined as neuroplasticity.

Neuroplasticity is the human brain's ability to change and adapt based on life experiences, our thoughts, and the circumstances we encounter. Also, suppose these experiences and thoughts are repeated sufficiently. In that case, our brain has the power to make new nerve connections to associate the thoughts and the behavior and situation and convert these connections into habits.

So, you see your emotions become part of you. When we hate something, our brain connects that hatred to everything related to that something. The best thing is that the reverse is also correct. If you can change your hatred into love, then too, your brain will make love-based connections, which, in turn, become habits. It is our choices that create good or bad habits.

Therefore, it is possible to train your mind to think positively and create good habits in your life. Consequently, emotions like anxiety and insecurity will find no place in your life.

Positive thinking is not a vague theoretical concept found only in manuscripts. The effects of positive thinking are many, and numerous studies prove its efficacy in the following benefits:

- Lower depression and anxiety rates
- Improved physical and mental well-being which, in turn, has the power to increase your lifespan
- Lowered stress levels
- Improved coping skills during difficult times

While science still has not understood why positive thinking has so many benefits, there is little doubt that if you engage in positive thinking, you can harness the advantages mentioned above and more. Here are some highly implementable ways to train your mind to have positive thoughts.

CHAPTER 3:

Seeing Possibilities

Once you have experienced some success with this step-by-step guide to assist you with your depression and anxiety, you'll be able to make positive associations between past experiences and current beliefs. These positive associations will help you dispel the false talk that keeps you from moving forward and enjoying a future free of depression and anxiety.

What Are Positive Associations?

Positive associations are when you take two or more objects or feelings and connect them.

Likewise, you can learn to make positive associations with your feelings and something positive. Without intending to, you have come to make negative associations with your sense of depression and sleep. You know that you can escape depression by sleeping. When you begin to feel depressed, you automatically want to curl up and sleep to relieve the depression. Wouldn't it be fantastic if you could make some positive associations that would allow you to change your thinking? For instance, you also know that exercise helps to alleviate stress and anxiety. So, when you begin to feel depressed, it would be so much better if you automatically wanted to get active. It's an association that offers physical and emotional benefits.

At first, the positive association feels much like you are rewarding yourself for feeling depressed, but this isn't the case. You're creating an opportunity to link something positive to do that will occur automatically, taking the place of the automatic negative self-talk and need to isolate.

How Do You Create Positive Associations?

Creating strong positive associations doesn't happen right away. To make connections that can change your behaviors and perceptions requires lots of practice, repetition, and an intentional routine. The positive motivator should also be something you love, which makes you feel incredible, free, and happy.

The longer you have suffered from depression and anxiety, the more frequently you will need to create positive associations to change your behavior and perceptions. Don't wait until you are in the middle of a deep depression to apply positive associations. Work on replacing the negative with positive when you're feeling good. If you are having an especially good day, use your journal to write down a description of the day. File in your mind how good it feels to be mentally strong and healthy. Enjoy the weather, and think to yourself how you're going to remember how warm and cozy it felt to enjoy the sunshine and be out in nature. When you start feeling down or begin to hear negative self-talk, give your mental files a going through, and search for those positive memories.

If your subconscious doesn't know the difference between imagined feelings and real emotions, then keep believing you're enjoying that incredible day. Think about how it felt to walk in the sunshine or lay in a hammock on the beach. Remember what it was same to take that dream vacation with your loved one. Smell the salt in the air, and feel the sand beneath your toes. Soon, your mind will focus on positive thoughts and associations rather than the negative ones. Your mind will focus on what you tell it to, so make your automatic "go-to" thoughts be the positive ones.

Once you've got your ideas headed in a positive direction, you'll need to follow that up with immediate action. Don't just think about something positive; do something positive.

Rewarding your positive thoughts with positive actions will keep the associations healthy. Merely distinguishing the behavior cannot be the association or the reward. Sometimes the reward is not to change. When you've experienced depression and anxiety most of your life, you could just be too darn comfortable with your feelings. You have accepted that you are a rather sad and anxious person, and then you think about ways to justify your feelings.

CHAPTER 4:

Noticing Beauty, Benefits, and Blessings

Putting in the effort to heal yourself from troubling emotions like depression and anxiety only matters if you will continue putting in the effort to maintain your wellness. If you immediately stop practicing your wellness approach when you start experiencing relief from your symptoms, or if you throw in the towel when you do not see the results you desire, you can guarantee that your results will not come.

The following Practices Are Things You Can Do to Maintain Your Mental Wellness on an ongoing Basis:

- **Regularly Assessing Your Approach**

   As you continue the path of healing yourself from depression and anxiety, you must regularly assess your approach and make sure that you are having the best impact on your overall health that you possibly can.

Reassessing your approach consistently allows you to ensure that you are always using the best approach possible and that you are making significant improvements regularly.

- **Integrating supportive Practices**

As you integrate these supportive practices into your life, make sure that you consider how they impact you. Remember, you are your primary focus here. Hence, you always need to consider your thoughts and feelings when engaging in any behaviors intended to support your healing. Pick activities and self-care practices that genuinely fill you up and make you feel good about yourself. There is no shame in having a self-care game that looks completely different from how the "standard" self-care game looks or incorporates practices that were not listed above. As long as these practices are genuinely healthy for you and promote your mental (and physical) wellbeing positively, they are likely a great addition to your self-care routine.

- **Seeking Support When It's Needed**

Just because you have decided to engage in self-healing does not mean you are immune to needing support. Support is an invaluable tool that can make your self-healing practices far more effective and efficient. Learn how to ask for support when you need it and teach yourself how to find nutritional support. This is the way to help you experience tremendous success with CBT.

- **Having Empathy for Yourself**

  Being empathetic towards ourselves does not mean being complacent, either. Your goal is not to let yourself off the hook for not taking positive action towards healing. Instead, it is to remind yourself that, sometimes, the results do not look as you wish they would and, sometimes, they take longer to achieve than you expected. This does not define that you are a failure or that you are not worthy of healing. It merely means that you are having a hard time with your genuine and immense emotions.

- **Continually Educating Yourself**

  Continually staying educated on how you can lead a healthier mental life and assess your thoughts for supporting you is the best way to make sure that you are always equipped with the knowledge you need to keep your mind healthy. Be sure to read up on mental health, stay focused on keeping your general health up, and educate yourself on the experiences you may have if your depression, anxiety, PTSD, anger, or procrastination is retriggered.

  Regular education can help you stay clear on the warning signs and regain control over your mind before experiencing a sizeable problematic episode that can support you in staying clear of your disorder altogether.

- **Eating a healthy Diet**

  When you are experiencing anxiety and depression, staying on top of your dietary habits is not always easy. It is not uncommon with both conditions to avoid often eating because you genuinely feel as though you are not hungry. The reality is that you are hungry; however, your increased stress has resulted in your appetite being suppressed so that the energy that would be used to digest food can instead be used to manage your symptoms of stress.

- **Drinking Plenty of Water**

  Like food, many people who are experiencing anxiety or depression will also forget to drink a healthy amount of water on a day-to-day basis. Dehydration is another factor that can escalate the number of stress hormones being produced within your body. It can produce troubling symptoms that can worsen your mood, such as headaches. Increasing your water intake and ensuring that you consume three liters of water every day can help you stay healthy and keep your body happy. Water is essential in supporting your brain, making up 73% of water to function healthily.

- **Maintaining Your Hygiene**

  Personal hygiene is another part of our daily routine that tends to be overlooked when experiencing intense anxiety or depression. Simple activities like brushing your teeth or hair or taking a shower may seem pointless when experiencing depression. You may find yourself feeling as though you lack the energy to stand up long enough to get the job done, so you simply avoid it altogether. Avoiding personal hygiene is unhealthy for you, but it also worsens your mood and leads to you having an increased likelihood of remaining depressed or anxious.

- **Caring about Your Looks**

  Caring about your appearance does not define that you have to be vain or that you have to apply makeup or put hours of effort into your appearance. Instead, it merely means that you take the time to clean yourself up and dress up nicely so that you look as though you care about yourself. When you behave as you care, your mind begins to recognize this and produces the feelings of caring too.

- **Getting regular Activity**

  Physical activity is not only great for supporting a healthy body, but it is also great for supporting a healthy mind. When you participate in a regular activity, you allow yourself to release any built-up energy that may be lingering in your body and producing feelings of depression or anxiety. Ideally, you should join in at least 30 minutes of intentional physical activity daily or about 200 minutes per week.

- **Relaxing on Purpose**

  Relaxing on purpose gives you time to unplug and tune out from the world around you. During this time, you want to release yourself from the pressure of the world and give yourself the freedom to just "be" with no strings attached. Suppose you have a big family or find yourself living in a home that is not relaxing for you. In that case, you might consider engaging in some other form of relaxing activity regularly. Going to a spa, sitting at the park, attempting float therapy, or engaging in other solo activities can be extremely helpful.

- **Getting proper Sleep**

  Rest is powerful, and unfortunately, many people do not get proper sleep every single night. When you are depressed or anxious, you might find yourself feeling extremely tired regularly. You might even find yourself sleeping more often than not, potentially causing you to wonder why you are still so tired despite getting plenty of rest. The reality is that when you are down or anxious, your mind is often too stressed out to allow you to experience real and deep rest. Instead, your sleep is typically light and restless or filled with nightmares that result in you feeling stressed out and uncomfortable in your sleep.

CHAPTER 5:

Cultivating Positive Feelings

Doing the things, you love is an essential part of beating depression. It would be best if you did those things that energize you and put you in a good mood. It would be best to learn how you could manage your stress and lead a healthy lifestyle simultaneously. It would be best to practice setting a limit to what you can and cannot do. Your day should not only be about work. You should set some time aside for fun activities to refresh your mind. Of course, you cannot forcefully have fun, but at the same time, you can always push yourself to do things that you love and know will bring a smile on your face.

Doing these things might not lift your depression all at once, but you will be feeling better and upbeat. When you are out there in the world, your mood will automatically get lifted. Pick up something you used to love before. You can also choose creative fields and express yourself in the form of writing poems or painting. You can also compose music if that is something you love. You can also read manuscripts or journals, watching movies, or cooking your favorite food. If you have pets at home, you might as well spend more time taking care of them, or you can play with them in an open space to relieve your depression. Take a day vacation to someplace new, or you can also hike up a nearby mountain. You can go on a picnic with your friends as well.

Indulging in activities does not mean you have to do something physically active. You can nap because having enough sleep is also essential if you want to fight off depression. Sleep problems and depression often go hand-in-hand. You should not sleep too much because both sleeping less and sleeping more can adversely affect your mood. Learn some healthy habits of sleeping and don't fall back. It would be best if you had a fixed time of going to be and waking up for starters because this will help keep your sleep cycle in check. In case you are taking naps in the afternoon, limit them to 15 to 20 minutes only and not more than that.

Stress is a significant factor when it comes to depression. So, you need to figure out all those things in your life that add up to your stress. It can be anything like money problems or even unhealthy relationships. Regain control of your life by finding ways to relieve the stress. Avoid burnouts by creating a balanced schedule. You can also try practicing gratitude because it is quite helpful. If you think that you are being overloaded with your routine, take some time off to appreciate everything you have in life.

It would be best if you are also familiar with relaxation techniques as they turn out to be quite helpful. You can practice yoga or meditation every morning. Or, you can also go to a spa or have a long, hot bath at home. Everyone has their way of relaxing, and you need to find the one you are comfortable with.

CHAPTER 6:

Creating Challenging Goals

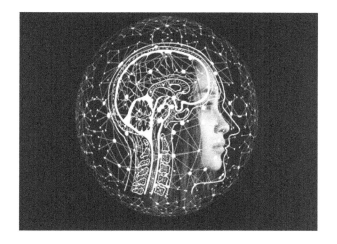

The Importance of Developing Goals

Goals play a crucial role in helping us to move forward in our lives. They are essentially the oxygen that our dreams and aspirations breathe. They are the beginning steps on the adventure we take and our last in the path of achieving success. It's vital to truly realize the significance that setting goals have on all our lives.

Goal Setting Is Crucial Because...

Any planning you do to prepare and set yourself up for success in the future is a goal. From planning our chores to developing a retirement plan and everything in-between, the small tasks, we do every day help set ourselves up for a brighter tomorrow.

Provides Us with Focus

Do you think you could shoot an arrow without a target to hit? If there were nowhere to aim, you would just aim at a random object to strike. Why would you choose to aim at random, and what would the purpose behind it be? Exactly.

The bow and arrow example is a literal analogy to how life would be without goals. Even if you have the potential and drive, without focus, your talent and abilities are useless.

Sunlight cannot burn through a magnifying glass without focus, and the same goes for you. You will be unable ever to achieve anything unless you focus on your efforts.

Your goals provide you with a direction in your life. When you have a clear sense of direction, this allows your mind to hone in on your target. Instead of wasting time and energy aimlessly shooting, this gives you something to aim for and hit, a.k.a. reaching your goal.

255 | P a g .

Provides a Way to Measure Progress

When you set goals, you are paired with a system to measure your overall progress since you are equipped with a benchmark to compare it to. For instance, say you have a goal to write a novel that is 300 pages in length. You start to write each day and strive to work hard in doing so. Then, you lose track of how many pages you have written and how many more you must write to reach your quota. Instead of freaking out, you can simply count the pages you have done, determine the progress, and figure out how much you still need to write.

Keeps Us from Becoming distracted

When you set goals, you are also providing yourself with mental boundaries. When there is an endpoint in mind, you are better at avoiding distractions and remaining focused on the result. This occurs automatically. No matter who or what meets you along the path you are treading to get to your goal, it always stays locked in and insight. This is why successful individuals thrive on setting goals to stay automatically locked in and give their goals 100%.

Help Defeat Procrastination

Setting goals creates a kind of personal accountability. Goals have a way of sticking in your mind, and if they go uncompleted, they do not just go away. You have probably had that "Shoot, and I was supposed to do _____ today!" moment several times in your life. This is your brain's way of reminding you to get back on track. They also help you to overcome laziness.

Give Your Motivation

Goals are the root of inspiration and motivation. They are the building blocks to the foundation for your drive to complete things in life. When you make a goal, you create an endpoint to aim for and get excited about. It provides you with the only thought of accomplishing it, which develops the motivation you need to keep up the momentum to get it done.

Goals are tools that give you the energy to focus in a positive direction and are easily molded to fit your priorities when they change. They can connect you directly with your innermost desires, which help motivate you and provide you with something to achieve.

Gives You the Reins of Your Life

The majority of society in today's world is sleepwalking their way through life. Even if they are working hard, they do not ever feel a sense of achievement, which is derived from the fact that they fail to set a sense of direction.

When you fail to set goals, you are spending your life running up and down endlessly without achieving anything. You are merely just fulfilling the goals of others, not yourself.

Setting goals centered on your desires helps you break out of the autopilot many of us are in and genuinely start living consciously. Don't let others inform you of what to do. This is your life that you should be taking charge of in a proactive way. Goals help you to think for yourself and then go out and get what you want.

Gives Us Ultimate Results

All of the most successful people in the world set clear and concise goals, from athletes to business professionals to performers and everyone in-between. When you can set goals, then you have the vision to work forward. You are then ensured that pushing yourself will lead you to achieve better results, rather than just lying around waiting for things to happen.

When actions can be measured, there is significant room for continued improvement. If you fail to specify your targets, you will find that things will never really get better because there is nothing to work towards, even if you are working your butt off.

When you are setting goals, thinking ahead is the key to create an actionable plan. Even when things do not go according to that plan (and they will trust me), you then have a system to recall and adjust your way to achieve those goals, since you are steering toward the vision you have for your life.

Makes Us Have Laser Focus

When your life's purposes have a good sense of direction, your goals can provide you with the focus you need to know precisely how you should be spending your energy and time.

This energy is the input that is necessary to create any kind of output. When you have a goal, you can make a focal point to place your energy to make a maximum reward.

Gives Us Accountability

Goals make you accountable. Instead of just talking the talk, you are now obligated to walk the walk. This sense of accountability is essential with you, not anyone else. No one else knows the goals you create for yourself to accomplish. When you set specific targets, you are better able to stay the course.

CHAPTER 7:

Finding Purpose

Along with new thought patterns, you want to include new behavior to get yourself back on track for a thriving social life. You need to organize and prioritize your life. Old patterns and habits will not craft new behavior and thinking.

You must change things up a bit; that means re-evaluating your life and weighing the good and the bad. What can you do differently that hurts you, or what can you do more that makes you feel better?

Start with creating a healthy routine that is not just in terms of food; try an early morning routine to start with a walk or a workout session in the morning. Even yoga could be extremely beneficial for someone who is fighting with depression. Something that gets the muscles going and the body up and energized instead of slow and sluggish is what you need.

Maybe even start with a good breakfast and conversation, or while watching a motivational clip. Start your day off the right way and with clear and positive thinking.

Sometimes, some habits and methods become ingrained into our very own existence even though they aren't healthy for us. It's only natural when suffering from depression that we look for relief and outlets for our pain.

But we must be conscious of the outcomes that these outlets may lead to. Slowly begin to pull away from your old habits and change your thinking about them. Let go of the false notion that you need these habits to survive or that you can't stop it because these habits overpower your mind. You must know and believe that you do not need those habits to eradicate them.

While slowly pulling away from these habits and old thinking methodologies, try embracing new habits and new thinking processes. Try hobbies and outlets that you may have shied away from before; perhaps you weren't ready at that time. Right now, is the time to be happy and try new things and discover new places.

When stuck in the same job and daily schedule, life can become quite tedious and monotonous for us, with the same events happening repeatedly. At such a time, life doesn't sound that appealing, right?

When trying to heal from depression, the last thing you need is boredom and thinking that things are just as they are and never change or get better. This is a false narrative painted by depression, and you have to rise above it, change things, and not drown in the daily circle of stress.

Now, having your routine and new activities that you like to do are all important, and you should take time to think about activities that you want to do and how you want to get them done. But also prioritize the things in your life from the most important to the least. Identify your goals from your wants and your needs.

Ask yourself what needs to be done and what can wait. This will help you prioritize and organize your life systematically.

The structure is something that helps to keep us grounded, and so is having a foundation. When you are aware of what you want out of life and when you have a purpose, it gives you a sense of inspiration; a reason, if you will.

We are all on this earth trying to find our place, which drives us to do what we do. Some people want more prominent and happier families. Others want money and wealth. It is quite natural for wants to differ from person to person.

You must find your "want" and establish what place it holds in your life. Are you want a healthy priority or something that gets in the way of what is right for you?

Nothing is perfect, and yes, we can't plan out every facet of our lives. But we can perform our best to be prepared for unforeseen occurrences. Having the affairs in your life fall into place will help in your transforming into the new you. These steps will aid in your recovery and healing.

This transformation process is a beautiful time when your mind is experiencing an unparalleled awakening. You may glance in the mirror and look new to you. Remember that this is not a bad thing.

Changing and evolving is something to look forward to, for how are you to know your true potential if you don't change and try new things? If you don't, that could be equated to confining yourself in a box.

Step outside that box and recall what you see in your world. You cannot change something that you do not even know exists. So, seeing your actions and thoughts from an outsider's viewpoint is beneficial for becoming a new person with a new mental structure.

Now, think about a time in your life that caused you tremendous stress, an event that perhaps led you into depression.

Do You Think about It?

Now expand on that. I want you to remember all the activities and everything that led up to it. Pick apart the memory and decipher what you could have done differently. Think about the decisions you made and think about why you were in that state of mind.

Once you reach a genuine conclusion as to why things happened the way they did, you'll have a firmer grip on your future. You will then become more seasoned in making the right choices.

Now, of course, you are still in the same body, so you are still you. But you can have new thinking and a wiser outlook in life. That alone can make you a new person. You can overcome depression and obtain happiness through your new self. This all starts from within. This new thinking will help you move forward in your life.

CHAPTER 8:

Cherishing Relationships

Relationships can be hard work. The good news is that adopting a more mindful way of life can strengthen your relationships, help you resolve arguments, and generally feel happier around other people.

What Does a mindful Relationship Look Like?

At the start of your relationship, you were probably mindful of one another. You were on your best behavior. You tried to impress them with your kindness, humor, and devotion. Your priority was to keep them happy, hoping that they would stick around. When you were apart, you probably thought about them all the time.

Unfortunately, once we've settled into a relationship, we often start taking our partners for granted. Other concerns, such as work or starting a family, start to take up more of our attention. No honeymoon period lasts forever, but you can keep your relationship intimate and fresh by committing to mindfully loving your partner. So, what does this mean?

A mindful relationship looks like this:

- Both parties feel respected.

- Both parties feel as though their partner truly listens to them.

- Both parties know that their partner is interested in them as a person.

- Both parties know that their partner finds them attractive.

- Disagreements are handled sensitively but directly.

- Both parties understand that relationships require ongoing maintenance if they are to succeed.

Sounds good, doesn't it? Mindful relationships aren't perfect, but they are far more satisfying than sliding into the kind of rut that many of us know all too well.

Communication: The Key to successful Relationships

Poor communication causes resentment and misunderstandings, which can ultimately ruin a relationship. All too often, we don't bother to check that we've understood what someone else is saying. Or, even worse, we don't listen properly in the first place. For instance, are you guilty of using your phone or reading a magazine when a partner or friend is trying to talk to you? If so, you're putting your relationship in jeopardy. Your loved one probably feels disrespected and resentful, which isn't a reasonable basis for love or friendship.

How to Be a great Listener?

When was the last time you talked to somebody who listened to what you had to say? Someone who gave you their full attention, listened mindfully, and never interrupted? These folks are rare – and popular! They tend to have lots of friends, and they enjoy satisfying relationships. Visualize how much better your relationships will be when you start interacting mindfully with others.

Mindfulness Exercise: Mindful Listening

1) When someone tries to start a conversation, you need to decide: Can you give them the attention they need and

deserve, or would it be better to delay the conversation? If it's the latter, ask if you can talk after. Explain that you want to listen to what they have to say, and you'd instead not multitask.

2) When it's time to have the conversation, stop whatever you're doing, and pay attention.

3) Maintain eye contact.

4) Try not to think about what you're going to say ahead. Wait until another man has finished speaking before thinking of a response. Often, we fall inside the trap of becoming distracted by our thoughts or judgments. This prevents us from appreciating what someone is trying to tell us.

5) Hold back when it comes to giving advice. If someone asks for your opinion, then give it, but be aware that they might just want a chance to vent.

6) Try to maintain an attitude of compassionate curiosity. Until you have evidence to the contrary, assume that the other person is acting with positive intent.

Listening is a crucial skill for mindful arguing. As you know, mindfulness helps develop impulse control and patience, which could make all the difference to the outcome of a fight.

During tense conversations, pause — if only for two or three seconds — before responding to a provocative statement or question. Be kind to yourself. Acknowledge that you are in a tough spot and recognize any anxiety or anger that comes up. Rehearse answers in your head before speaking aloud. It's far better to take your time than say something you'll sooner regret. If you feel overwhelmed, excuse yourself for a couple of minutes to think through your options.

Judgments

Do you judge others? You're in good company. Almost everyone does it; it's just human nature. We also tend to jump to conclusions about someone else's behavior, even when we don't have much evidence to support our beliefs.

For example, you may notice that your partner has left some crumbs on the kitchen table, and you automatically say to yourself, "They're so messy and lazy." Or maybe they have been late home twice this week, so you jump to the conclusion that they must be having an affair or that they want to avoid spending time with you.

When we start passing judgment on everyone else's behaviors, we get into trouble. We get so caught up in reacting to what they've said or done — or what we think they've done or said —— that we start acting irrationally.

We don't have to get swept up in our judgments. Instead, we can choose to be mindful when they pop up. No matter how compelling your emotions, try not to assume that they are a true reflection of reality. When you find yourself angry or upset at someone else, take a few deep breaths, and pay attention to what you are thinking and feeling. Notice each judgment. Imagine it as a bubble floating away on a breeze or a leaf in a stream flowing past you.

This takes practice. Judging others, whether or not we admit it, can feel good. Self-righteousness can give us a kind of energy and even boost our self-esteem. You'll never get rid of your impulse to judge people, but you can use mindfulness to limit its effect on your relationships.

CHAPTER 9:

When to Search for Professional Help

One of the first criteria for selecting a therapist is whether or not you like the person. Do you feel comfortable? Do you imagine that you could talk about difficult things and cooperate with this individual? There has to be that feeling of esprit de corps, or you will be wasting your money.

Where to Begin?

It can be quite helpful to ask all the professional people in your life if there is a particular therapist that they know or would recommend. Ask your minister, accountant, attorney, massage therapist, beautician, barber, and physician. Carefully take down the name and pertinent details, as well as a note about who referred you to that person, as you will want to mention that when you first meet.

If there is a particular characteristic that you need to have in your therapist, a Google search might bring forth some possibilities. If, for example, you require a particular location, insurance acceptance, or expertise in something definite, such as adult giftedness, sexual abuse, sexuality, or alcoholism, it could be easier to find someone with an Internet search.

Follow up on each possibility with an e-mail or phone call and make an appointment. You will decide rather quickly upon meeting the person whether or not it might be a fit, but either way, take along your list of questions about the arrangement's suitability. Does this therapist practice Cognitive Behavioral Therapy? What are the therapist's educational background and credentials? Any specialties? What professional organizations does that therapist belong to? What insurance is accepted?

Types of mental Health Professionals

Any mental health professional may be well-equipped to help you with CBT.

In other words, her primary title maybe something else, like a clinical social worker.

It is unlikely that you would find a person who is strictly a cognitive-behavioral therapist without those skills being in the context of a broader profession.

Some of the Professions that Might Also Offer CBT Are as Follows:

- Psychiatrist
- Psychologist
- Master's level counselor (marriage and family therapist)
- Social worker
- Advanced practice nurse

Depending upon your personal preferences, you may be interested in a type of help that is not licensed, such as the following:

- Spiritual counselor
- Hypnotherapist
- Life coach
- The Initial Sessions

The first session will be a consultation; in which you decide whether or not you wish to continue with that person. You will want to ask about the therapist's values and orientation to determine the presence of like-minded compatibility. It will be essential to discuss costs, insurance, and the estimated length of the course of treatment.

Limitations of Family and Friends

Although those closest to you are highly interested in your life and experiences, they may not be the best source for advice or support. Undoubtedly their perceptions are skewed, and they may even be threatened by your hopes of making significant changes in your life. It might be a better use of your resources to turn to people who can efficiently zero in on your difficulty. Those are the people in your inner circle who know you very well and could perhaps push your buttons when making significant efforts to change your life. Just be careful about what you disclose.

CHAPTER 10:

Living the Life, You Imagine

Happiness is a choice. Whether we like it or not, problems can exist. The question is, will you allow your circumstances to define you, or are you going to decide to be fabulous no matter what you are dealing with? Focusing your attention on negativity, or the people who project it is a waste of time and energy. Having the right perspective provides you with the ability to enhance every area of your life.

Find Your Personal Source of Joy

Joy is an absolute necessity for our overall wellbeing. Look deep within and discover what personally makes you happy. What motivates you to go on, to become a better person, to wake up in the morning? No matter how you perceive your way of living, there is something that you are passionate about, or you wouldn't be reading this.

Accept Your Individuality

No one on this planet has the same DNA as you with the same fingerprints or bone structure. You are unique! Most of the time, depression and anxiety comes from comparing yourself to other people. You feel like you are not enough, that you don't fit in, you don't fit a particular ideal of beauty. Whatever the case may be, such negative thinking will cause you to remain stuck in life, and you will have a hard time moving forward. Your aim should be to become the best version of yourself, and if you spend time developing yourself, your skills, talents, and abilities, you won't have the time or energy to compare yourself to other people.

Volunteer

Until you get involved in other people's struggles, you will continue to believe that you have got the worst problems in the world. There is suffering on every corner, and if every capable person were to offer a helping hand, the world would be a better place. Unfortunately, this isn't the case, and human beings are selfish; they only think about themselves and forget that some people would wish to be in their situation. The easiest way to become a volunteer is to join an organization such as a local church. Most likely, you will be able to get involved in feeding the homeless, going to hospitals, or visiting older adults. Once you realize that life isn't that bad, you will start to appreciate what you have.

Gratitude

Living a grateful life is essential to a positive mindset and living a happy and healthy life. Depressed, anxious, and negative people tend to focus on what they don't have. This is what they think about continuously, and it becomes a mantra for their lives. As you have learned, the more you think about something, the quicker it will manifest in your life.

 This then leads to a pattern of your circumstances confirming what you believe, and you begin to experience the downward spiral of decline.

Exercise Your Mind

The brain is a muscle, and if it doesn't get any exercise, it will become limp and unhealthy, just like a body that doesn't exercise. Here are some ways that you can exercise your mind daily:

- Learn a new word
- Solve a math problem
- Do a crossword
- Play a memory game
- Read something informative
- Brain training exercises

Remember, everything starts in the mind. It is your most valuable tool. The more you invest in it, the stronger it will become.

Remember that You Are Not alone

This journey that you have started is not an easy one. There are going to be days when you just feel like throwing in the towel. When this occurs, reaching out to someone is important, don't try and fight this fight alone. Whether it's an accountability partner, your doctor, or your psychiatrist, make sure that you make that phone call when you feel like things are getting too much for you.

Eat a healthy Diet

The majority of people don't realize how important the mind is, so whether knowingly or unknowingly, they abuse it. The assumption is that a healthy diet only has benefits for the body; however, a growing body of evidence suggests that it is just as crucial for the mind. According to the Mental Health Foundation, a good diet is essential to mental health. The foundation also suggests that diet can play a role in the prevention, management, and development of certain conditions, including:

- Alzheimer's disease
- Attention deficit hyperactivity disorder (ADHD)
- Depression
- Schizophrenia

There is no suggestion that diet can control these conditions; neither should patients stop taking medication nor embark on a healthy eating regime. However, diet can play an influential role when combined with other treatments while managing these conditions. The conclusion is that eating a healthy and balanced diet contributes to feelings of well-being. A healthy diet consists of foods containing the right minerals, vitamins, proteins, fats and carbohydrates, and plenty of water.

Pay Attention to What You Read, Listen to, and Watch

You will often hear people mention that some manuscripts are 'pulp fiction' or 'trash.' They refer to manuscripts that are easy to read and don't challenge the mind. Reading like this every so often is not going to harm, just as much as eating a hamburger every once in a while, won't affect your health. However, eating junk food every day is terrible for the body in the same way that was reading pulp fiction every day is terrible for the mind.

It's worth spending some time thinking about your mind diet every so often. Ask yourself the following questions:

- How good or bad is your mental diet?
- What are you consuming more of? Films, videos that challenge the mind, or reality TV and pulp fiction?
- How does this impact you?
- Are there any improvements you should make for your mental diet?

If you are struggling to build a sound mind diet habit, think about someone you admire and study their habits.

Surround Yourself with the Right People

You must remove all negative people out of your life. This sounds very extreme, but it is essential to your mental health. We have all heard the saying, "You can choose your friends, but you can't choose your family." This is indeed true, but if you do have opposing family members, which you probably will, you are going to have to keep them at arm's length. People fail to realize how much power family members can have over them. You will realize that there is a lot of emotional blackmail in families, and it becomes difficult to free yourself from them if it means that you have to save up some money and move out of a home that is what you are going to have to do. Your emotional stability is more critical than a nagging mother who wants you to stay at home so she can have someone to complain to all day!

Enjoy Life

What do you enjoy doing? Do you like to travel? What are your hobbies? When we take part in doing something that we love, we emit positive emotions which will attract the happiness and joy you have been looking for. Whatever it is, make sure that you find time in your schedule to do indulge in it. Remember, you only live once. Living a life of misery and sadness isn't worth it. Make a career out of doing what you enjoy and pay attention to how much you flourish when you get to do things that please you.

Conclusion

Depression that is left untreated can get worse over time. Although it would not be just to question the sanity of a depressed person as there are millions of depressed individuals that can lead everyday lives, there is no question that if depression is not dealt with appropriately, the mental state and ability to function normally can be drastically impacted. As the spouse or partner of a depressed individual, there is value in putting energy into working towards maintaining your sanity and the sanity of your spouse or partner.

The goal is to equip you with the ten tips that you can use to maintain your mental health in the context of a relationship with a depressed individual.

Tip 1. Understand that this Is Not Your Battle to Face, but Your Partner's

By recognizing that the depressed person needs to take the lead in addressing their depressive illness, a partner allows that person to exercise the agency that comes with being a functional, competent adult. Still, they also are taking an essential step towards maintaining their sanity. In other words, recognizing that this condition is not your own but someone else's is not only a matter of respect but a pragmatic step towards a healthy mental attitude. Although taking a back seat may be difficult, it is essential for both you and your partner.

Tip 2. Seek Help from those Around You, including other Family Members and Friends

This supportive role is one that you can share with those around you. Although some depressed individuals are in the difficult position of going through this situation with no support, many depressed persons are fortunate to have family around to lend a helping or supportive hand. For you, what this means is that there are people around you that can help. Although every person has the right to privacy, including a depressed individual, it is not wrong to inform your family that you are dealing with a difficult situation in your relationship and that you may need some support of your own. You do not have to disclose all of the details if you feel unnecessary or inappropriate. This simple step of looking to your friends and family for support can make a huge difference in maintaining your stable peace of mind.

Tip 3. You Should See Your Role as Someone Helping Your Partner Through Depression

Being a supportive partner means that you show compassion to your partner, you show understanding and tolerance for what they are going through, and you are there when they need you. It does not mean that you bombard them with your wants and needs regarding their depression. Taking a supportive role may be difficult for some people, but doing this is not only crucial for your partner, but it is also essential for your mental health. Taking the lead in situations like these can be exhausting, stressful, and unnecessary. Give yourself a mental break and assume the role of the supporter.

Tip 4. Be aware that Your Partner's Depressive Symptoms Can Cause You to Start to Feel Depressed Too

You need to understand that a nearby person and a relationship with the depressed person should be conscious of your feelings of sadness. At this stage, you should know the criteria that psychiatrists use to diagnose depression and the warning signs of depression.

Tip 5. Be clear About What You Can Take in the Relationship and What Represents Crossing the Line for You

Limits and boundaries are necessary for every relationship. As a spouse or partner, you feel what you can take and what you cannot take from the other person. This is a useful and essential step to take in all relationships because it promotes the general good feeling (and sanity) of both people in the relationship. By having a sense of what you need from the other person (or what you need the other person not to do) and communicating these, you allow both of you to understand what is expected and healthy for the two of you.

Tip 6. Work with a Therapist, Both as a Couple and as Individuals

Psychotherapy is an excellent option for depressed individuals because it can treat depressive symptoms and improve their relationships with others. Partners should avoid using therapy to change their partner into what they want them to be. The example of a partner writing a list of changes that they want from their partner and telling their partner to give it to the therapist comes to mind. The therapy is not for you. It is for your partner. The assumption here is that your partner is dealing with major depressive disorder, not you, and the therapy is for their benefit.

Tip 7. Do Not Neglect Your physical and mental Health during this Process

The point here is that part of maintaining your sanity in a depressed partner's face is to take steps to maintain your health. That means taking time off and getting better when you are sick, going to the doctor when you need to go to the doctor, and the like. If you neglect your health as your partner deals with their depressive illness, then you may find yourself at risk for developing a severe illness or less able to deal with the vagaries of depression. You will be a more effective supporter of your significant other if you take care of your mental and physical health.

Tip 8. Make sure to Focus on the Things that Make You Happy Like Exercise, Writing, Cooking, or whatever Pastimes Bring You, Joy

The story of depression does not have to be dominated by low mood and lack of interest in the activity. Perhaps depression is contagious because the depressed person's people find themselves behaving as if they have anhedonia. Suppose you want to maintain your sanity when you need to think about what makes you happy and engaging in them. This is not intended merely as a distraction so that you are no longer thinking about your partner's depressive illness; this is a crucial step to keep you feeling happy and healthy.

Doing things that make you happy gets all of the positive endorphins pumping in your body. These endorphins will cause you to feel happier than you may be at the time, and they may even cause your ailments to improve if you are sick. And, hey, if you are lucky, these happy feelings and endorphins may just be contagious for your partner.

Tip 9. Consider Finding Encouragement from Self-Help Journals

The reality is that you may need to take it a step further when it comes to maintaining your sanity during this difficult time. You may need to put effort into helping yourself with the aid of self-help journals. Although some people have an opinion about self-help journals and may feel that they do not need them, the reality is that millions of people have found help from these sorts of journals. If you find that the other tips listed here are not enough for you, invest time in other resources that may provide you with the help you need.

Tip 10. Try Not to Take the Behavior of Your significant other Personally

When you love someone, it may be difficult not to take the things they say and do personally. Depressed men and women have little quirks that make their condition difficult for them and trying for the people around them. A sympathetic person understands that their significant other is going through difficulties, and they can separate the person from the depressive illness. Still, it is not always easy to do this. Also, every person has a breaking point. A partner who has been cycling through depressive episodes may cause their significant other to lose patience with them for an extended time. The goal here is that you do not lose patience with your significant other but continue to demonstrate sympathy for what they are going through.

Part Six:

Cognitive behavioral Therapy

CHAPTER 1:

What Is Cognitive Behavioral Therapy?

Think of yourself as a slate that has so many words, images, and texts scribbled over it in a way that makes it impossible to make sense of anything. You cannot tell where one text starts and where the other ends, but you are sure that they are all linked together in a way, but you just can't figure out how. If you were confronted with such a board, you would be saddened by its current state. It is not like a puzzle that you already have a clear picture of what the end product is meant to be. To make sense of this slate, you would have to get to the root word or foundational phrase. When you find that foundation, you may have to erase individual words and replace them with suitable alternatives; in sum, it is only as you piece each new word that you begin to see a semblance of normalcy. This process is what cognitive-behavioral therapy encompasses.

When you find yourself acting, thinking, and speaking in ways that you ought not to due to excessive anger, crippling anxiety, overwhelming depression, and an upsurge of negative words, it would be impossible for life to make sense. This is because everything you do would be filtered through these emotions. It would seem as though everyone in the entire world is out to get you. Every step you take would seem to be steeped heavily in led. Little events spark up rage in you so volatile that it would seem you are carrying a little hurricane on the inside of you that is spinning everything out of control and destroying everything in its path. And it doesn't matter if it is raining outside or the sun is shining so bright since you have your thunderstorm complete with thick dark clouds and heavy showers that are programmed to flush out any happy thought or feeling. No wonder you feel the way you do. Your slate is wholly messed up. With Cognitive Behavioral Therapy (CBT), you start to understand why you feel the way you do. It is only in answering why you can determine how you can tip the scales in your favor. You did not wake up overnight and began to feel the way you do. Even if your condition is inherited, you have established several behavioral patterns over time that cause these conditions to set in. With Cognitive Behavioral Therapy, you can identify those behavioral patterns and offset their influence by deliberately replacing them with better behavioral practices that are more suitable. However, it has also been known to treat long-term ailments like irritable bowel syndrome, controlled by better eating behavior.

However, it is essential to note that Cognitive Behavioral Therapy is not designed as a curative measure. Far from it. Instead, it helps you cope better with those conditions by effectively helping you take control of your emotions. For CBT to work, you will require the following in equal measure:

- Consistency
- Diligence
- Willingness
- Honesty

The goal is to help you establish new behaviors to manage anger, anxiety, depression, and negative thoughts. They say that it takes 21 days to develop a new habit. But that is not the reason we (you and I) are working with 21 days. Simultaneously, specific behavioral elements can be introduced to reverse the experience and bring you to a place where you can better cope with whatever is happening.

These daily exercises are straightforward, but the effect is powerful. Some must be conducted repeatedly to affect. However, if done right, you can notice a significant difference from the first try. Others must be combined in specific scenarios for maximum impact, and I have carefully pointed those out as well. To get the desired results, you must be deliberate in taking each action. It also helps to curate your experience post the action. This would help you put things in perspective and give you some insight into problematic areas. There is so much going on in your life right now, and none of it is probably making sense.

We (you and I) are using Cognitive Behavioral Therapy to retrace your steps, realign your behavior with the emotional results you are hoping to achieve, and generally bring you to a place where you are emotionally balanced and content in who you are experiences you have in life. Because let's face it, life will always have those terrible and unfair incidents happen to us even though we are not quite deserving of those situations. But we don't have to let those incidences define us. When we root ourselves in our true identity, we will not be quickly phased by what happens outside. There will be moments when you will slip. And that fall will discourage you from going forward. A momentary slip is not the end of the world. This is what makes you human. The part that makes you extraordinary is choosing to get up from that fall, but the pieces that were broken apart and resolved to be stronger for it. You are made of more, and over 21 days, you will discover just how amazing you are!

CHAPTER 2:

Cognitive Behavioral Therapy for Depression

Restructuring

Challenging your thoughts is going to be the most powerful tool. Like anxiety, look for the factual data and analytics of a situation to put some logic into your thoughts. When we can look at the factual data that can be numerically measured, it can be harder to have depressive thoughts about our situation. It is not about just being grateful for what you have but instead looking at the positive things in your life rather than emphasizing the negative. Always ask yourself real questions and test the evidence that you have for a particular prediction. This isn't going to make you feel better right at that moment. However, if you start this combative of automatic thoughts right now, it will get better every day. You have to be patient and willing to put that time in.

Combating Thoughts

Now that you have some Cognitive Behavioral Therapy tools, you have to look at yourself as a warrior fighting against the cognitive distortions. You are holding a shield, and you have to fight off all the distortions your mind is throwing at you. Sometimes, they might still slip pass, but it is up to you to keep them from destroying you. It might seem impossible, but you should always combat your negative thoughts as they come toward you.

Humans are obsessed with labels. Not just ones that come from a label maker, but more general ones, like good/bad, fat/skinny, ugly/pretty, useful/useless, smart/stupid. We like to put things into one category, especially if you are someone with depressive tendencies and polarized thinking.

Look at the Root

When using CBT, you want to go back to that time a specific event took place and think about why that event or comment affected you so. Sometimes, when a person states something related to our insecurities, it can be a form of validation, good or bad. If you think you are not intelligent and someone makes a small joke about your smartness level, it can cut pretty deep, even though it wasn't meant to be hurtful at all. This is because it is an unspoken validation from the other person that our deepest and darkest thoughts are right, even though that wasn't the other person's intention.

Remember that small instances are just that. Though they might have become defining moments, they don't have to anymore. Most of the time, if you ask a person about certain small instances that stick with you, they end up not even remembering that they said that in the first place!

Journaling

Expressing your feelings is an incredibly effective way to overcome your mental illnesses. Holding things in can be like a plastic bag or even a boat. If you put too much in, it is going to sink or break. The same can be said with your mind. If you are not adequately healthily expressing your feelings, it will take a toll on your mental and physical health.

Journaling is entirely subjective. Everyone's mind is different, and that means their journal should be as well. What you decide to put in your journal is up to you. The main idea is that it should be an expression of your emotions, recording of your different feelings, and a go-to for helpful reminders or a guide to overcoming anxiety and depressive thoughts. You can go back and look at to see different information to help you continue in your recovery.

Quantitative Data

Some people aren't creative or have trouble expressing their emotions, and that's completely fine. They might not be able to write full entries. Writing might be awful to you, and the sound of it alone gives you anxiety. That's completely fine.

Look at your journal for answers that aren't always easily identifiable. Even if you are creative, this method of journaling can still help as well. You could aim to implement both, but it is up to you to figure out what works best with managing your depression at the end of the day.

Writing Letters

Sometimes, we stay quiet in situations that require us to speak up because we don't know how to process our emotions. One way to change this is to write letters. This can be a part of your journal, or it can be completely separate. Maybe you write one to yourself at five years old, and one when you are fifty. Write a letter to yourself yesterday, angry that you weren't able to get as much work done as you hoped. Write one to your ten-year-old self, letting that kid know that it was OK they didn't make the volleyball team or that it wasn't their fault their parents fought all the time.

Write one to yourself in the future. Tell yourself how much you have thought about them and how you hope they are doing well. By doing this, you are expressing emotions that you have kept inside. Other times, you might want to write letters to other people. Maybe you are angry, so you write down everything you hate about them. While it might be hard to go through those feelings, it can be incredibly therapeutic to get your thoughts out.

Unraveling

When unraveling, you have to make sure that you are looking at the cause and effect of different cognitive distortions. One end will be the cause, and the other end will be the effect. When you have it all raveled together, it can be hard to process. When things are laid out correctly, you will see easier the things that upset or frustrated you.

What you have to unravel is going to be different for everyone, but some necessary steps can help you do this:

- Identify the symptom of anxiety. What is it that has made you decide to use CBT?
- Pick out what cognitive distortion might have led to your symptoms. Do you often deflect? How are you framing the issue? Are there moments of catastrophizing?
- Reflect on the issue and see the ways they've grown roots and spread. How have they affected other parts of your life?
- Look to your past to see what might have caused the issue in the first place. Was there a specific trauma, or did you experience prolonged abuse?
- Come up with a solution for resolving this issue. Which method of CBT is going to be the most useful for you to overcome it? Sometimes, unraveling will be enough in itself, but you have to use multiple methods other times.

This is just a straightforward method of unraveling. It starts with the issue and ends with a solution. Though it looks easy, it won't always be that simple to carry out step five, the recovery methods. However, looking at it in these simple steps can help ensure that you are logically looking at your anxiety and depression.

CHAPTER 3:

Cognitive Behavioral Therapy for Insomnia

Insomnia

Insomnia is a sleep disorder that makes it difficult for a person to fall asleep or stay asleep and, in some cases, causes you to wake up early and be unable to fall back to sleep. Because of a lack of proper sleep, a person usually feels tired after waking up. Insomnia disorder is terrible because it saps out your energy, affects your mood and health, and your work performance.

Enough sleep varies from one individual to another, but adults' recommended sleep is seven to eight hours of sleep each night.

At a certain point in most adult's lives, a person may experience acute insomnia that can last for several days or weeks. However, some people suffer from prolonged periods of chronic insomnia. This type of insomnia may be associated with other conditions that need medical attention.

With simple daily habits, one can overcome insomnia and go back to enjoying healthy sleep patterns. How does a person know they have insomnia? Insomnia has various distinct symptoms. These may include:

- Finding it difficult to fall asleep during bedtime
- Losing sleep in the halfway through the night
- Getting up very early
- I am feeling tired even after a night's sleep.
- I am feeling tired during the day and sleepy.
- Being irritable, anxious, and depressed
- Finding it hard to be attentive, focused on assignments, or remembering.
- Having a higher rate of mistakes and accidents
- I am always worried about sleep.

When Should One See a Doctor?

If the lack of sleep is so severe that you find it hard to function in your day to day activities, seeing a doctor is advisable. The doctor should work with you to identify the cause of insomnia and develop various treatment options. In case the doctor feels that you are suffering from a sleep disorder, he may recommend you see a sleep specialist.

How Age Relates to Insomnia?

Insomnia can be directly related to one's age. The older a person gets, the more they experience insomnia. When a person gets older, they experience:

- Your sleep pattern changes — as a person ages, sleep becomes less. Slight noise or other changes in one's environment can cause a person to wake up frequently. Age causes the internal clock to advance, making one tired earlier at night and waking up even earlier. Regardless, it is healthy to have the same amount of sleep when older, just like a younger person.

- If you are less active during the day, changes in what you do may take an afternoon nap. This, in the end, will interfere with your sleep at night.
- Change in health — if a person experiences chronic pain from conditions like arthritis or back pains, they may have challenges sleeping. Other conditions, like anxiety or depression, also interfere with sleep. Other medical issues may cause frequent urinating at night, such as bladder problems, diabetes, among others. Restless leg syndrome and sleep apnea are also other conditions that interrupt sleep patterns.
- Prescription drugs — older people use more prescription medicines than younger people do. This increases the chance of developing chronic insomnia.

Insomnia can affect children and teenagers, as well. However, most of the causes at this age is due to their irregular patterns in their sleep schedules. Lack of sleep can also be associated with some risks in specific individuals.

The Risk of Suffering from Insomnia Is more significant if:

- The individual is a woman. Shifts in the hormones during the menstrual cycle or menopause play a significant role. When a woman is going through menopause, they experience hot flashes and night sweats that will interrupt sleep. Pregnant mothers also experience insomnia due to hormonal changes.

- If you are over the age of 60, then your chances of suffering from insomnia are high. As you age, you experience changes in health, increasing the risk of insomnia.

- If you are experiencing a mental health disorder or a physical health condition, you are at a greater risk of developing insomnia.

- Stress is another condition that increases insomnia. When a person is undergoing stressful situations, they may have temporary insomnia. However, prolonged periods of stress may also result in chronic insomnia in many individuals.

- Lack of regular schedule is another contributor to insomnia. A person that often travels across different time zones or works with various shifts is likely to experience insomnia.

Insomnia Complications

Just like having a healthy diet is essential, having healthy sleep patterns is also essential and regular. Regardless of the reasons causing your lack of sleep, insomnia can physically and mentally affect you negatively. Individuals with insomnia have a lower quality of life as compared to individuals that enjoy good sleeping habits. Various complications associated with insomnia include:

- Poor performance at work or school
- Decreased reaction time on the road that may result in higher risks of accidents

- Mental health disorders like anxiety, substance abuse, and depression
- Higher risk of long-term diseases such as heart diseases.

Practical Strategies that Will Help You Sleep better

Developing good sleep habits can help prevent insomnia and cause a person to enjoy a sound sleep. Some practical things you can do to improve your sleep will include:

- Be consistent in your bed and wake time even during the weekends.
- Be active. Regular physical activity will aid in promoting good night sleep.
- Check your medications if one of the side effects is lack of sleep. If so, speak to your doctor to switch the medicine.
- Try and avoid daytime naps, and if you feel you must, limit the duration.
- Limit or avoid the use of nicotine, alcohol, or caffeine entirely.
- Avoid taking huge meals before bedtime and taking of sugary beverages.
- Don't use your bedroom as a work station or a place for entertainment. Use it only for the intended purpose.

Come up with a relaxing bedtime ritual, like taking a warm shower, listening to soft music in low volume, or reading.

CHAPTER 4:

Cognitive Behavioral Therapy for Anxiety

S trong emotions arise before thoughts related to them are fully formed, not afterward, as it likely appears when you look back on an incredibly emotional incident. As such, you will often find that it is easier–and more effective–to change how you feel about a situation than what you think about a situation. As such, if you want to use CBT to help your anxiety, then the following exercises are a great way to work on calming your feelings directly:

Focus on how Your Feelings Change

When working with CBT, it can be easy to get so focused on the way your feelings are currently aligned that it can be easy to forget that feelings are fluid, which means they are always open to change, even after you have already put in the effort to work on them for another specific reason. Likewise, just because you spend a month or more working on your feelings of anxiety, it doesn't mean that you aren't still going to get a little anxious now and again. Instead, it is essential to take the new anxiety in your stride and see how severe it ends up being before you get too stressed out about it, possibly causing yourself far more mental strife than you would have had you just taken the small amount of anxiety in your stride in the first place.

You may also find it helpful to verbally acknowledge how you feel in the moment and how you expect those feelings to change once the anxiety has passed. For example, you might say, "Currently, I felt a little anxious, which is natural given the situation. When the feeling passes, I anticipate feeling clear-headed and calm once more."

Additionally, you may find it helpful to keep a close eye out for the first signs that the feeling is passing, and the anticipated change is about to begin. Not only will focusing on the anxiety being over actually make the end come on sooner, but it will also stop you from reacting poorly to the anxiety at the moment. Feelings always shift, and keeping this fact in mind may be enough to push things in the right direction.

Act Normally

While Generalized Anxiety Disorder is considered a mental illness, anxiety itself is a useful survival tool when doled out in moderation. It is only when things get out of hand that it goes from being helpful to harmful, sort of like an over-eager guard dog. The truth of the matter is that your anxiety response only kicks in because your body responds to the current situation as if there was a threat. Regardless of whether the threat is real, a perceived threat is enough to set off the response.

As such, one way to train your anxiety to be selective effectively is to give it the type of feedback it understands so that it knows it is not currently needed. Anxiety takes its cues from what you do along with a primary type of emotional pattern matching, which means that if you act as though everything is currently standard, then the anxiety will back off and calm down. As such, you will want to do things such as maintain an open body posture, breathe regularly, salivate, smile, and maintain a calm and measured tone of voice.

Suppose you can successfully adopt just one of these behaviors when you are feeling stressed. In that case, you can successfully alter your feedback enough that your fear response, directly from the sympathetic nervous system, receives a message that says everything is fine. One of the most common ways of mitigating an oncoming feeling of anxiety is to chew gum. If you don't have any gum handy, only miming the act of doing so is going to be enough to make you drool, convincing your body that nothing interesting is going on.

The reason that this is so effective is that you would never have the luxury of eating a delicious meal during times of severe crisis, which makes your body naturally assume that nothing that taking place is a legitimate threat. This, in turn, changes the feedback loop the body was expecting and causes the anxiety to retreat into the background. Just knowing that you have this quick trick in your back pocket can give you a boost of confidence that takes you past the point where your anxiety would trigger in the first place.

Remember, anxiety functions are based on the expectation of something catastrophic happening shortly. All you need to do is prove that this is not the case, and you will be fine.

Discover underlying Assumptions

As a general rule, if you feel anxious about a specific situation, then this is because you are afraid of some potential consequences that may come about as a result of whatever it is that is taking place. However, if you trace those fears back to their roots, you will often find that they aren't nearly as bad as you may have assumed, they would be when they were just a nebulous feeling of anxiety.

For example, if you are anxious about attending a party, then looking inside to determine the consequence you are afraid of might reveal an internalized fear of meeting new people. Tracing that fear back, you might discover that it is based around the consequence of other people not liking you, which you are determined to avoid due to issues in your past.

However, if you trace the consequence of people not liking you, then you may find that it makes you upset because it reinforces existing feelings regarding your general likeability. Once you get to the ultimate consequence that is causing you anxiety, you can look at the problem critically and determine what you can do to solve the issue that you are avoiding. In this instance, reminding yourself of people who do like you is an excellent way to avoid the issues you are afraid of.

This exercise is also incredibly useful for those dealing with relationship issues, as they can clearly describe all of the fears, they have associated with the relationship falling apart. In the process, they will understand that things will continue as usual after the relationship falls apart and move on if the relationship is not intact.

Progressive Muscle Relaxation

Another useful technique in combating anxiety is known as progressive muscle relaxation. This exercise involves tensing and then relaxing parts of your body in order. This is because the body can't be both tense and relaxed at the same time. Thus, if you feel an anxiety attack coming on, a round of concentrated tense and release exercises can cut it off at the source.

Progressive muscle relaxation exercises may be done routinely or before an anxiety-provoking event. Progressive muscle relaxation techniques may also be used to help people who are experiencing insomnia.

To get started, find a calm, quiet place that you can dedicate to the process for approximately 15 minutes. Start by taking five, slow, deep breaths to get yourself into the right mindset. You are going to want to apply muscle tension to a specific part of your body. This step is going to be the same regardless of the muscle group you are currently focusing on. Focus on the muscle group before taking another slow, deep breath and then squeezing the muscles as hard as you possibly can for approximately five seconds. The goal here is to feel the tension in your muscles as fully as possible, to the point that you feel a mild discomfort before you have finished.

Once you have finished tensing, rapidly relax the muscles you were focusing on. After five seconds of tensing, let all of the tightness flow out of your muscles, exhaling as you do so. The goal here is to feel the muscles become limp and loose as the tension flows out.

It is crucial that you deliberately focus on the difference between the two states; this is the most crucial exercise. Remain in this state of relaxation for approximately 15 seconds before moving on to the other group of muscles.

CHAPTER 5:

Cognitive Behavioral Therapy for OCD and Intrusive Thoughts

In recent times, OCD has become somewhat of a common term in everyday society. The word is often thrown around lightly as a tease to someone who likes things a certain way or feels the need to be orderly and tidy. Most of the people who do this, however, don't even know the first thing about OCD or how serious it is.

Obsessive-Compulsive Disorder (OCD) is a chronic mental condition affecting more than 2.2 million individuals in the United States. It is defined by distracting and disturbing thoughts, pictures, or impulses that often cause someone to participate in repetitive, ritualistic, or mental conduct. Understandably, those suffering from OCD feel a great deal of anxiety about their illness because they feel like they are slaves to their obsessions and compulsions. It can also make it difficult for a person to think about it.

Another challenge that a lot of OCD patients struggle with is overcoming their need to enact their obsessive thoughts into compulsions. OCD is driven by anxiety, and people with this disorder often wrongly believe that the only way to alleviate their anxiety is by giving in to their compulsions. While it does provide some relief, it's a maladaptive solution to a much more complex problem, as it can take away an individual's sense of control and free will over their lives.

In the early days of psychotherapy, OCD was one of the most prevalent mental disorders globally, but most psychologists didn't have the faintest clue on how to treat it. Many of them simply resorted to psychodynamic therapy, behavioral therapy, and antidepressants, even though it was proven to have little to no significant effect. Fortunately, in 1966, psychologists discovered the first effective psychosocial intervention for OCD: exposure and ritual prevention (EX/RP). EX/RP is a CBT technique that proved to be so successful in treating the disorder that it went on to inspire the development of other similar treatments, most of which with successful outcomes. Now, Cognitive-Behavioral Therapy (CBT) and its specialized techniques are considered the "golden standard" in treating OCD patients and alleviating their anxiety. It also helps them manage their obsessions and decrease their compulsions, which adds to better life quality. So, if you're suffering from OCD and looking to CBT to help you manage your condition better and ease your troubles, then you've come to the right place. But first, let's go over the different kinds of obsessive thoughts and compulsions.

Among the most common obsessive thoughts include themes of:

- Orderliness and symmetry — People with this kind of OCD often worry about the neatness and tidiness of everything

- Contamination — This lead someone to fear being contaminated with germs and bacteria
- Rumination — This means imagining a mistake that one has done or might do
- Checking — This type of obsession leaves the person wondering if they've already turned off the lights, turned off the stove, locked the doors, etc.
- Dark Thoughts — This induces a fear of even thinking about "sinful" or evil things
- Violence — A person with these thoughts often fears harming others, even though he/she does not want or intend to

As for compulsive behaviors, among the essential kinds are:

- Skin-picking
- Hair-pulling
- Hoarding/collecting
- Repeated hand washing or cleaning
- Repeating particular words or phrases
- Performing certain tasks repeatedly
- Constant counting

As you can see, OCD can have many different subtypes and symptoms, depending on the individual's particular obsessions or compulsions. But more often than not, effective treatment for one type of OCD is sufficient for the rest as well. There is also the degree of the severity of OCD that needs to be put into consideration.

CHAPTER 6:

Using CBT to Beat Procrastination

Several factors lead us to procrastinate. Once we understand these factors, we'll consider the many tools that CBT offers for breaking this habit.

Do You Have a Procrastination Problem?

People vary in their tendency to procrastinate and in the specific tasks they put off doing. Take some time to consider ways you might delay doing things you know you need to do. Do you find yourself in any of the following situations regularly due to procrastination?

- Realizing you didn't leave yourself enough time to finish a task by the deadline.
- Feeling inadequately prepared for meetings.
- Trying to force yourself to do a task.
- Being stressed about time as you rush to appointments.
- Trying to hide that you haven't been working on a task.
- Producing lower quality work than you're capable of.
- Telling yourself, "I'll take care of that sooner."

- Waiting to feel more inspired or motivated so you can do a task.
- Finding ways to waste time instead of doing what you need to do.
- Relying on last-minute pressure to complete a task.

Let's begin by considering why we procrastinate and then turn to ways to overcome it.

What Drives Procrastination?

We've all been there — a paper to write, an errand to run, a home project to start, or any number of other tasks we put off. Little good seems to come from these delays — for example, procrastination is associated with worse academic performance and more significant sickness. Nevertheless, we often struggle to take care of things in a timely way. The following factors contribute to our tendency to procrastinate:

- Fear that it will be unpleasant: When we think about doing a task, our minds often go automatically to the most unenjoyable parts. If we imagine cleaning the gutters, we think about wrestling with the ladder. When we consider writing a paper, we dwell on the struggle we'll have at times to express our ideas clearly.

- Negative reinforcement: Every time we put off a task, we think it will be unpleasant. We experience a feeling of relief. The brain interprets that relief as a reward, and we're more likely to repeat an action that led to reward. In this way, our procrastination is reinforced. Psychologists call it "negative reinforcement" because it comes about by taking away something seen as aversive. In contrast, positive reinforcement is when getting something we like strengthens a behavior — for example, receiving a paycheck reinforces our job's behavior. The negative reinforcement from avoiding a task can be tough to overcome.

• Is there any task you've been meaning to get to and keep putting off, or that you routinely delay doing? Which of these factors applies to your procrastination tendencies? In your journal, write down any ways in which you've been procrastinating and what seems to drive it.

Is Procrastination Always a Bad Thing?

Some researchers have suggested that procrastination's benefits should not be overlooked. For example, procrastinating gives us longer to come up with solutions, and can also allow us to harness the pressure of a deadline to energize our efforts. Management professor Adam Grant cited the benefits of procrastination on creativity in his writings. According to Dr. Grant, our initial ideas tend to be more traditional. Giving ourselves additional time can lead to more innovative solutions, which we never reach if we finish the task as soon as possible. These potential advantages need to be weighed against the stress, missed deadlines, and lower quality work linked to procrastinating.

Strategies for Beating Procrastination

Understanding what causes procrastination gives us clues as to how to break out of it.

Because multiple factors lead to procrastination, we need a wide range of tools to choose from to overcome it. These tools can be divided into three domains:

- Think (cognitive)
- Act (behavioral)
- Be (mindfulness)

Over time, you can find a set of strategies from these three areas that work well for you. Some conditions can make procrastination mostly likely.

Depression saps our energy and motivation, making it hard to take care of things.

Individuals with ADHD struggle to meet deadlines due to difficulty focusing on a task and low motivation to complete it.

Anxiety disorders can also lead to procrastination — for example, and a person might delay writing an e-mail due to fear of saying something stupid.

Think: Cognitive Strategies

Much of our procrastination comes from how we think about the task and our willingness and ability to complete it. Strategic changes in our thinking can weaken procrastination's pull.

Acknowledge that You Probably Won't Feel like Doing It Sooner, either

We might assume we'll get to a task once we feel like doing it. Though, the truth is that we probably won't want to do it after any more than we want to do it now. We can stop waiting for a magical time down the road when it's effortless to do the task.

Challenge Beliefs about Having to Do Something "Perfectly"

We often put off starting a task because we've set unrealistically high standards for how well we must do it. Keep in mind that it doesn't have to be perfect; it just needs to be done.

Choose the Think strategies that resonate with you and write them in your journal to practice when needed.

Being on Time

Being late reflects a specific type of procrastination, namely a delay in moving ourselves from one place to another by a deadline. Follow these principles if you want to improve your punctuality:

Be realistic about the time required. Time how long it takes to reach your destination. Be sure to factor in time for incidentals like saying goodbye to your family and giving yourself a buffer for the unexpected (e.g., traffic delays) so you don't underestimate the actual time required.

Be careful about setting your clock or watch ahead to help you be on time. This strategy often backfires because we know our watch is fast, and we can disregard it altogether.

Avoid starting an activity close to time to leave. Beware of trying to squeeze in one more activity before leaving for your destination, even if you think it will take "just a minute." There's a good chance it will take more time than you have and end up making you late.

Bring things to do in case you're early. If you're afraid of being early and then wasting time with nothing to do, bring a journal or some other enjoyable or productive way to pass the time if you're early.

CHAPTER 7:

Using CBT to Overcome Jealousy

Ending jealousy is like altering every mental or behavioral response. It begins with consciousness. Awareness lets you see that the predicted stories are not real in your head. If you are so straightforward, you no longer respond to the possibilities your imagination might imagine. Jealousy and anger are emotional reactions that are not true in believing situations in your head.

You should change what you think affects what your imagination projects and remove these harmful emotional reactions.

Even if the reaction is warranted, envy and rage are not good ways to cope with the situation and get what we want. Trying to change anxiety or resentment when you feel like trying to control a car skidding on ice.

Your ability to deal with the situation is much improved if you can clear the risk before we get there. This means addressing the beliefs that cause jealousy rather than trying to control your emotions. Dissolving relationships permanently means changing the underlying beliefs of fear and unconscious expectations of what the partner is doing.

The Steps to end jealous Reactions Permanently Are

a. Recover personal power so that you can control your emotions and stop reactive behavior.

b. Identify the core convictions that trigger the emotional response.

c. Be mindful that your convictions are not valid. This is distinct from scientifically "knowing" that the claims are not real.

d. Gain power over your focus so that you can actively select your mind's story and emotions.

Several factors establish the envy dynamic. Practical solutions will tackle multiple elements of values, experiences, feelings, and strength of personal will.

You will leave the doors open to those negative emotions and behaviors if you lack one or more of these components.

You can step back from the story by practicing some simple exercises and refrain from the emotional reaction.

You can do it if you want to change your feelings and actions. It only takes the readiness to acquire adequate skills.

Principle Triggers of Jealousy Are Convictions Which Create Insecurity Feelings

Low self-esteem is based on convictions of who we are. To eradicate fear and low self-esteem, we do not have to change our confidence in the false self-image. While some people believe this may be difficult, it's only tricky because most people haven't learned the skills needed to change their faith. When you practice your skills, it takes minimal effort to change a belief. You just stop thinking about the story. It takes more effort than it does to believe something.

Self-Judgment May Intensify the Feeling of Insecurity

It is not enough to "learn" the emotion intellectually. Only in this way will the Inner Judge abuse us with criticism of what we do. The Interior Judge could use this knowledge to push us into more vulnerability by an emotional downward spiral. You will need to develop skills to dissolve beliefs and falsified self-images and to control your mind projects. The practices and skills of the audio sessions are available. The first and second sessions are free and should give us an idea of how the mind works to create emotions. Sessions 1 and 2 also give you great exercises to regain some personal power and adjust your emotions.

One of the steps to changing behavior is to see how we create the emotion of wrath or jealousy from our minds. This very step will allow us to take responsibility and puts us in a position to change our emotions.

We don't take responsibility if you're in a relationship with a jealous partner and want to change your behavior to avoid envy. Saying things like, "when you wouldn't, then I wouldn't react like this." This kind of language flags a powerless attitude and attempts to control your behavior by dealing with it.

How the Mind Produces the Emotions of Anger and Jealousy?

I described in the description below the mechanism of jealousy and anger. When you try to overcome envy, you probably already know the complexities I explain. This explanation can help to fill the holes in how the mind turns knowledge into self-judgment and increases low self-esteem and insecurity. This theoretical understanding will contribute to the development of consciousness to see these complexities when you do so. But you need a different set of skills to make significant changes. You don't have enough details about how you build your emotional reactions. Just like realizing you have a flat tire; you didn't know how to patch the tire because you stumbled over the screw. I will use a guy as a jealous companion for the example. I am talking about different pictures in mind, and you can refer to the chart below or see the Relationship Matrix for a more detailed description of these images.

Compensating for Fear

To overcome the emotion created from the hidden false image, he concentrates on his perceived positive qualities to counteract the emotion created by his secret image. The man creates a more optimistic False Image of himself from these attributes. I call this the Projected Picture because he needs to be seen like this. The mental consequence of a positive self-image is not self-rejection or indignity. There is greater acceptance, and he generates more love and happiness. Notice that he has not changed; depending on the moment, he only has a different image in his mind.

The hidden image belief causes unhappiness, while the projected image causes more pleasant emotions. It must be remembered that both pictures are fake. Both images are in the mind of the man, and nobody is him. He is the one who creates and reacts in his imagination to the images. In his imagination, he's not an image.

The mind of the man blends the projected image with the qualities attracted by women. The characteristics are often considered positive because women are attracted to them. When a man receives attention from a woman, he links himself to the projected image instead of "not good enough." The increased trust in the projected image leads to more social acceptance, love, and happiness.

324 | P a g .

CHAPTER 8

Using CBT to Beat Addiction

A mind that has been ruined by drug addiction is the perfect breeding ground for negative thoughts and other emotional health issues. Managing challenging thoughts and emotions is hard enough for a sober person, but the experience is ten times worse when you consider a drug addict. Thankfully, drug addicts can benefit from CBT. Cognitive-behavioral therapy has been shown to achieve long-lasting results in the treatment of various addiction types.

The Following Are some of the Benefits of CBT in Addiction Treatment

- **Provides a Network of Support**

    Cognitive-behavioral therapy allows addicts to have a network of support, which is very crucial during the recovery phase. The average addict, if not given positive encouragement, could easily relapse into drug abuse. Therapists are there to offer positive encouragement and gently guide these people toward full healing. When addicts realize that no one cares about them, they are likely to go back to seek solace from drugs. Having a network of support is critical for avoiding relapse and ensuring general emotional well-being. People are social beings. Thanks to the support network, addicts have someone to talk to.

• **Increased positive Thought Patterns**

Addicts often struggle with a negative thought pattern that makes them feel helpless, ultimately making them go back to doing drugs. An addict struggles with many bleak thoughts and feelings. However, through the power of positivity, they can overcome their mental and emotional health issues. CBT emphasizes positivity. The more positive an individual is, the less likely they are to slide back into drug addiction. Therapists help addicts overcome their conditions by planting positive thoughts in their subconscious. This helps addicts become positive by default. And whenever they experience emotional troubles, they have someone to guide them.

• **Enhancement of Self-Esteem**

Low self-esteem is one of the reasons why people turn to drugs and alcohol. They want to forget their misery and helplessness. But cognitive behavioral therapy helps addicts develop a great self-image. As their self-esteem level goes up, they find less desire to escape reality through drugs and alcohol. They are happy to be themselves. Therapists constantly reinforce addicts' self-esteem and thus raise their desire of wanting a better life than the one they presently have. To get rid of an addiction, the affected person must want to change their circumstances, and this desire becomes natural when an addict's self-esteem is given a boost.

- **Learning to Resist Peer Pressure**

  Since we are social beings seeking peer acceptance, it is exceptionally challenging to resist peer pressure. It is challenging for the average person, and ten times more challenging for the drug addict. Cognitive-behavioral therapy equips addicts with the skills for overcoming peer pressure and focusing on their important life goals. When it comes to resisting peer pressure, they are trained first to imagine saying "no" to their peers, and then actually saying "no" within a controlled environment. By the end of the training, they won't have any difficulty saying "no" to both their peers and anyone else who might negatively influence.

- **Cost-Effectiveness**

  Cognitive-behavioral therapy is one of the most affordable addiction treatment methods. Some other treatment methods, like rehabs, have in-house arrangements for the patient. These treatment methods can be incredibly expensive. Cognitive-behavioral therapy can be conducted on an outpatient basis and achieve great results. Insurance plans even cover this treatment method. Cognitive-behavioral therapy is not one-sided. For its success, both the therapist and the patient must work side by side. If the patient is not cooperative, then the treatment will tumble down. Cognitive-behavioral therapy is not complicated. It involves general procedures that lead to the restoration of health. There are no expensive or complicated tools required.

- **Gradual Steps**

    Overcoming an addiction is no walk in the park. It is a time-consuming quest. Remedies that claim to offer instant results are misleading. In cognitive-behavioral therapy, a therapist introduces new principles to the patient as they advance through the treatment. There are principles set aside for the beginners and principles set aside for those who have reached the advanced stage. Walking through these steps, the patient's resolve is strengthened, and they are less likely to run back to drugs or alcohol than patients who have been through any other treatment model. The beauty of cognitive behavioral therapy is that it doesn't advertise itself as a quick fix. It takes real effort to achieve results. However, the effects are long-lasting.

- **Continuity of normal Activities**

    Cognitive-behavioral therapy is done on an outpatient arrangement. The patient is free to indulge in other activities for the rest of their time. This is unlike rehabs, where patients are held on campus, effectively suspending their daily engagements such as going to work. With cognitive behavioral therapy, patients are neither separated from their family nor do they have to seek leave. Because of its flexibility, more people are willing to take this treatment method. And if the sessions are scheduled at night, then your day will run without even a slight hitch.

- **Gradual end to Therapy**

    Cognitive-behavioral therapy places the entire focus on the patient. The concepts and exercises may be adjusted following how the patient is faring. In some forms of addiction therapy, the treatment lasts only for a specific time, and then it is cut off. This kind of arrangement doesn't take care of patients who would take ordinarily long to recover fully. In cognitive-behavioral therapy, the first few weeks are typically intensive. Still, as the patient's condition improves, the therapist finds less need to have intensive sessions and focuses on the patient's recovery speed.

CHAPTER 9:

Using CBT to Overcome Regret and Guilt

D o you ruminate about the mistakes you've made? Do you want to feel more comfortable with your past choices?

How Do You Feel about Guilt?

Everyone makes mistakes. We all have our faults. Even the kindest, most patient, and most moral of us have made poor choices. Unfortunately, hurting other people is part of being human.

CBT gives you the tools to understand where guilt and regret come from, how to move past them, and how to avoid making bad choices in the future. Remember, how you react to events – including your mistakes – is just as important as the event itself.

You Are Not responsible for Everything

If you are prone to guilt and regret, you probably have a habit of assuming too much responsibility. When you are too quick to say, "Yes, this situation is entirely my fault!" your view becomes warped. In reality, most unfortunate events aren't caused by one person. Life is more complicated than that.

For example, let's say that your relationship has recently broken down. You and your partner have fallen into a pattern of getting into trivial fights that turn into screaming matches. To make matters worse, you disagree on a couple of other issues, including the question of marriage — you want to marry, and they don't.

So, who is at fault in this story? If it happened to a friend, you would probably reassure them that there are many play factors.

Slicing the Responsibility Pie

The following exercise will help you step back from a problem or situation and understand the part you played in it.

Exercise: The Responsibility Pie

Make a list of everyone who played a role in the event you're feeling wrong about, such as a breakup or a fight.

Now, draw a large circle on a piece of paper. This is your Responsibility, Pie. Draw lines to divide this pie up into slices. Draw a slice for everyone on your list. Make the size of the pieces proportionate to their responsibility. Don't worry about getting the sizes or percentages exact. Go with your gut instinct.

Yes, but what if It Was My Fault?

Of course, you might have made a big mistake, and no one else is to blame. For instance, let's say you go to a conference for work, get drunk, and cheat on your partner with a colleague who doesn't know you aren't single.

Your partner finds out, and they end the relationship. In this case, your partner isn't to blame.

If you were to create a Responsibility Pie, the only name on there would be yours.

Exercise: What Are Your Beliefs About Guilt?

Complete the sentences below:

- "If I didn't feel guilty, I would…"
- "I don't think I can give up my feelings of guilt because…"

- "Guilt is useful because…"

What do you think your answers reveal about your beliefs?

Common Beliefs about Guilt & Why They Are So destructive

1. **"If I Feel Guilty, I Must Have Something to Feel Guilty about."**

   This is simply untrue. For instance, some people feel guilty when they survive an accident in which others died. This kind of "survivor guilt" is irrational. It's an example of emotional reasoning. Just because you think you are a terrible person who should be ashamed of yourself doesn't mean you have anything to feel wrong about. Only by stepping back and taking a long look at the situation can you come to a reasonable conclusion.

2. **"If I Feel Guilty, It Means I Am a bad Person."**

   Even if most people would agree that your guilt is justified, you are not the wrong person. This line of thinking is an example of generalization, which is a cognitive distortion. Like everyone else, you are a complex individual who has done great things and made mistakes.

3. **"Guilt Will Stop Me from Hurting People in the Future."**

Don't fall into the trap of assuming that guilt somehow protects you from repeating your mistakes. You might think, "Well, at least holding onto my guilt will make me think twice before doing something wrong!"

This approach is doomed to fail because it undermines your self-confidence. Your morals and values are better at helping you make good choices, not guilt. Guilt also damages your relationships with other people. It makes you averse and afraid, and your loved ones will always have the sense that your decisions and emotions are driven by something they can't see or understand.

4. **"I Need to Feel Guilty Forever because I Need to Punish Myself for what I've Done."**

In small doses, guilt is healthy. It's a kind of warning signal. Guilt lets you know that you've violated your moral code. When we feel guilty, we know it's time to make amends and apologize if appropriate.

Guilt becomes self-indulgent after a while. It doesn't always feel like a punishment. It can become almost comfortable. If you don't let go of your guilt, you'll build a self-image as a "bad person." You need to take responsibility for your past and how your feelings keep you stuck in place.

5. **"If I Let Myself Stop Feeling Guilty, this Means I Approve of My Actions."**

Have you ever been reluctant to forgive someone because you don't want them to let them off the hook? The same principle can apply to your guilt. On some level, you might think that allowing yourself to live guilt-free means that you are magnificent with the things you've done.

6. **"If I Make a Mistake, I Am an unacceptable human Being."**

This thought can be traced back to a single core belief: "I must be perfect, or I am worthless." This belief is both illogical and harmful. No one is perfect.

The sooner you realize this, the happier you will be. You wouldn't expect your friends and family to behave impeccably at all times, would you?

7. **"If I Keep Analyzing the Situation long enough, I Can Work Out Exactly How Much of the Blame I Deserve."**

Some of us want to know precisely what went wrong in a situation that left us feeling guilty. Unfortunately, the world doesn't work like that. There's no objective, scientific way to figure out exactly how much blame lies with us in most cases. It's smarter to invest your energy looking forward instead.

CHAPTER 10:

CBT and Mindfulness

As you can imagine, embracing positivity in everyday life can make a profound change in how happy and peaceful your overall life is. When you utilize a positive mindset every day, you will find that life, in general, tends to flow and unfold with more ease and that people in your life then start to respond to you in more optimistic ways.

While motivating yourself to maintain positivity every day is not easy, it is more than possible and certainly worth the effort.

First, positive people are almost always positive, no matter what, because of two key things:

They practice being optimistic about strengthening this capability further.

They choose to be positive because it feels a heck of a lot better than drowning in a pool of negativity.

We are not born positive or negative, and one person is not more capable of optimism from the other. Stop making excuses about your skills, challenges, or situations you are enduring regarding your level of optimism. There are no aspects that make positivity easy, even though many see it this way.

Positivity is primarily a choice. It would be best to have both free will and awareness to succeed and maintain a good sense of optimism in your life. Guess what? Every person, even you, is wired with free will and conscious awareness! You are always in the right place to be more positive and start reaping the benefits from it.

When you are aware of yourself and your life, you will then notice when you are starting to venture down the path of negativity. Having this awareness jumpstarts the choice between optimism and pessimism. Below are some terrific tips you can begin to practice to gain optimum results!

Mindfulness-based Cognitive Therapy focuses on cognitive therapy and mindfulness, rather than behavioral aspects from CBT. It looks at attitudes and mood, which is why it works well for people who find themselves in severe depressive states and suffer from unhappiness regularly. Breathing and meditation is a critical component of this therapy.

Mindfulness is about self-awareness in the same way that CBT is. Although CBT is hugely tailored around mindfulness, it involves analyzing and working on those things, which sometimes means we judge our thoughts and feelings. CBT also focuses on the behavior aspect and evokes change, whereas mindfulness raises awareness and believes that becoming aware can change without forcing it. Both concepts focus on the present and try to implement changes moving forward.

By adding mindfulness to cognitive therapy, we appreciate ourselves and show flexibility in our thoughts. There is growing evidence suggesting that MBCT can be a beneficial treatment for mental health issues, and it's often thought of being a great self-help tool (Edelman, 2006).

Important Ideas in Mindfulness-based cognitive Therapy

Mindfulness-based Cognitive Therapy focuses on emotions, thoughts, and attitudes. Basic ideas about MBCT are:

- It is building up a tolerance or coping mechanism that allows us to deal with painful situations better.
- I am open and non-judgmental.
- You are reaching an enhanced state of awareness.
- It is allowing us to gain insight into ourselves and being in touch with how we feel.
- Using meditation techniques to reflect, recover, and cope with specific situations. This can promote emotional wellness.
- We are incorporating breathing techniques to help us calm down and cope with our feelings and emotions.

Mindfulness-based Cognitive Therapy is aimed at those who suffer from heightened depression regularly. Its key components teach clients to break from those negative thought patterns and cope better while improving self-awareness.

How Does MBCT Work?

MBCT aims to try and prevent relapses of depression. If a person suffers from regular depressive episodes, it's essential to try and change this pattern. MBCT focuses on changing your relationship with your emotions. Mindfulness activities, such as meditation, can help to create balance and just like CBT. You can start to change your automatic negative thought patterns and replace them with new ones.

MBCT is about creating a routine and adopting mindfulness techniques to cope with an overwhelming situation. The hope is that you can replace your negative thought patterns and prevent those feelings of sadness from turning into depression (Psychology Today, 2019).

Problems that May Be addressed by MBCT

Much like CBT, mindfulness-based cognitive therapy is mainly used when treating depression, including moods and feelings of sadness. It has been recognized to help those suffering from anxiety disorders, relationship issues, pain, stress, and substance misuse. Let's not forget how useful these coping strategies are with panic too.

If you start to feel down, overwhelmed, or feel a panic attack coming on, the techniques involved in this treatment can prevent it from escalating into depression. However, this type of therapy is usually suggested under a therapist if you suffer from depressive episodes regularly (usually three episodes or more).

MBCT Techniques and Exercises

Below are some different techniques and exercises that you might want to explore as part of your MBCT routine. Remember, the routine is everything, so planning in time to breathe, meditate, or exercise is a great way to start your MBCT treatment.

- Breathing Exercises — Before you can meditate, you need to master your breathing. When we breathe, we typically use our chest, and we raise it and down as we inhale and exhale. Breathing from the diaphragm and stomach area is recommended with MBCT, which involves relaxing your stomach and allowing it to rise and fall as you breathe deeply. You may need to practice breathing daily, so spend some quiet time focusing on your breathing technique. You can lay back in the chair, close or open your eyes, or you may prefer to lie down.

- Guided Meditations — Many people learn to get themselves into a meditative state without being guided. Still, for beginners, there are many guided meditations you can use online, on channels like YouTube. Often, guided meditations focus on a specific area, but there are ones that focus on sadness and depression. If you're going to try a guided meditation, research the different ones available and listen to them for a few seconds until you find a soothing voice. Once you've found the one for you, kick back and relax. You should practice your breathing techniques for a couple of minutes, just before you begin.

- Walking Meditation — With any meditation, you need something to focus on, and in this case, you focus on your walking. You don't focus on each step or look at your feet, and you focus on the fact that you are walking. Walking is a great way to clear your mind, and because it's exercise, it allows you to refocus, and you will feel refreshed.

- Yoga Stretches — Yoga is an excellent exercise for mindfulness, CBT, and MBCT, as it is already a meditative exercise. There are different types of yoga, and some are more spiritual than others. Kundalini Yoga is meditation-based and involves quite a lot of breathing exercises as well as chanting. You can attend a class, or there are tutorials online, too, if you would prefer.

Other techniques from CBT, like journaling, are helpful for MBCT. Recording your thoughts shows that you're paying attention to yourself and your needs. It's a form of self-care which we could all do with a little more of.

MBCT is focused a lot more on positivity, so you could also think of daily things you are thankful for (Edelman, 2006).

Benefits of Mindfulness

As mentioned already, being mindful is a way to take care of yourself, and this has numerous benefits for your mind and body. This includes:

- Better general health and state of mind.
- Improved concentration levels.

- Insight into one's self and more in tune with emotions.
- Better control of thoughts and the ability to reason.
- Stronger problem-solving skills.
- Feeling motivated and positive.
- Decreased stress and anxiety.

Mindfulness Skills

Being mindful helps us to embed many skills that can help us in our life. It can help us process our thoughts more positively, as maintaining a fit and healthy outlook. As we feel happier and healthier, we take back control of our lives and are less likely to feel depressed, anxious, or stressed.

Mindfulness can help us to appreciate ourselves and understand the importance of caring for our mind and body. When we feel motivated and content, we can overcome barriers that hold us back. We can also feel rested and relaxed, which helps us to reason.

This means that we often live for the moment and live a happy, fulfilling life!

Conclusion

Indeed, CBT starts with a relatively straightforward way to understand a challenging situation and how we react to it. You have to remember that cognitive-behavioral therapy focuses on the three major components of a psychological problem: thoughts, emotions, and behaviors.

This simply means that when you experience a challenging situation, it is essential that you break it down into these components. When you break it down in this manner, you gain clarity about where to intervene and how to do it. In other words, if there is a chain of reactions of both behavior and emotional feelings that arise from having a particular negative thought, the best approach is to go back into reexamining the thought. However, if a negative behavior pattern seems to be the main problem, the wiser thing to do is learn a new response to the situation.

The truth is, there is no quicker way to fix your anxiety. It takes time and commitment for you to overcome your fears fully. When you go through cognitive behavioral therapy, it is essential that you face your fears head-on rather than trying to run away from them. This might make you feel worse at first, but it is only after that you can start feeling better. The most important thing is for you to try as much as you can to stick to your therapy and the advice given by your therapist.

Your pace or recovery may be slow, and this can be discouraging at the time, but you have to remember that it will be useful in the long-run. Therefore, rather than giving up, keep pressing on, and you will eventually reap the benefits. To support your therapy, you must start making positive choices. This includes everything from your level of activity to your social life and how that affects your condition. The best route is for you to begin by setting goals and making informed decisions that will boost your relaxation and functionality levels and offer you a positive mental outlook in your daily life.

Take time to learn about your anxiety so that it becomes easier to overcome it. Education is essential in ensuring that you know what it takes to get to the other recovery side. Right, that alone will not cure your condition, but it will help you make sense of your healing therapy.

Cultivate your support network to be isolated and lonely, as loneliness can make your anxiety even worse. When you establish a robust system of support from your therapist, family, and friends, you will significantly lower your vulnerability level. Make a point to see your support group frequently so that you can share with them your worries, concerns, and progress.

Also, remember to adopt a healthy lifestyle by engaging in physical activities and eating healthy foods. This regimen goes a long way in helping to achieve relaxation by relieving tension and anxiety. Therefore, in your daily routine, make it a point to schedule regular exercises. Also, refrain from foods and drinks that may make your anxiety worse, such as those containing caffeine or alcohol.

Part Seven:

Mindful Relationship Habits

CHAPTER 1:

Benefits of Building a Mindful Relationship

Importance of Relationships

There is ample evidence that correlations, often substantial, exist between quality and quantity of relationships and diverse outcomes, including mortality rates, coronary artery bypass surgery, immune system functioning, stress reactions, mental disorder, and life satisfaction. How have the mechanisms developed through which relationship events influence human biology? Some sources suggest that living and working in small, cooperative communities was the primary survival strategy for the human species since early humans were buffered by the social organizations from the dangers of nature.

Individuals are mainly psychologically attached to careers and intimates, and collaboration predominates among in-groups. Social interaction requires deciding what kind of relationship occurs, and hence the essential processes.

Relationships can be described in terms of the properties that define the parties' interdependence involved with how individuals change their conduct to comply with others' behaviors and desires. Therefore, persons in relationships respond (or not) to each other's desires, interests, skills, and emotional expressions; change their actions to be together (or not); delegate tasks to one another; react to each other's activities and circumstances, misery, and happiness; and take into account the fact of their interdependence in the organization of daily and long-term existence The belief that such patterns of reciprocal interaction are more insightful about relationships than abstract categories (e.g., partners, employers, friends) or basic static descriptors (e.g., length of association, existence or degree of effect) is fundamental to most conceptualizations of relationships. There is evidence of differential effects of the relationship contexts in many research areas. We then identify such areas to explain the importance of the psychological science of such evidence.

Personality and Social Development

Most personality development theories argue that maturity and aging are cognitive transition times, discontinuity, and earlier life habits transformation. It is assumed that these changes occur concerning the demands of the increasing biological status and social context of the person — the family, the workplace, and society in general. Thus, the development of personality is both a unique phenomenon and a social one.

For example, the young adult is expected to enter an institution that is, marriage and family — that will reinforce the community.

In such a relationship, the degree to which the essential need for intimacy at all levels physical, emotional, and others is fulfilled defines in most individuals the conception of the self as belonging or as alienated. The problem arises between the sense of generativity and the sensation of stagnation in middle adulthood. The person is expected to play the role of a participating, generative member of society at this point. Generativity may take the form of delivering the goods and services through which society functions or creates, rearing, and socializes future members of society. A sense of depression stems from the inability to develop a positive self-conception. According to Erikson, in adulthood, a conflict occurs over ego dignity versus the sense of desperation. At this stage, people realize they're reaching the end of life. If they have advanced successfully through the preceding stages of development, they will face old age with comfort in the feeling that they have led a complete life. Individuals lacking this quality in life frequently feel a sense of desperation for "wasted" opportunities.

During this time, critical life events include job choice, first work, marriage, and childbirth. The age range from 28 to 33 years reflects a transition from adult entry to the following settling period. The transition provides an opportunity for the young man to adapt and enrich the adult life's provisional framework that he created earlier. However, a moderate to a severe crisis is typical for most men; divorce and job changes are widespread during this period. There follows a settling-down period, starting in the early 30s and lasting until about age 40. During this time, the man's task is to become a full-fledged adult, underlines stability, and health. The individual makes deeper commitments to their profession, family, or whatever business is crucial to him. However, he also concentrates on "making it." This includes long-range preparation with a timeline for their achievement against specific goals. Many people focus on a critical event in life, such as promotion, as a symbol of society's ultimate affirmation.

The change to midlife lasts four to six years, peaking in the early 40s. This establishes a generational link between early adulthood and middle adulthood and reflects a beginning and end, a convergence of past and future, being part of both ages. A midlife change goal focuses on this gap between what is and what could be partly resolved. The transition may be relatively smooth, but significant instability is more likely to occur. The initiation period of middle adulthood starts at about age 45 and lasts to around age 50. Sometimes, the beginning of this new life structure is marked by a significant event in life, such as a change of job or occupation or a divorce or love affair. In other instances, the modifications are subtler.

Similarly, age-related traits are based on the socio-adaptation facets of personality, e.g., goal-driven behavior, coping styles, and life satisfaction. Consequently, it seems that how healthy adults communicate with the world can be constant, even though their roles shift with age. On the other hand, it revealed marked age differences in individual styles of dealing with the inner world of experience. For instance, 40-year-olds felt responsible for their environment, viewed the self as a source of energy, and were optimistic about risk-taking. Simultaneously, 60-year-olds saw the environment as challenging and even dangerous and viewed the self as passive and welcoming.

CHAPTER 2:

How to Build a
Mindful Relationship Habits?

One primary goal of mindfulness practice is to develop the ability to shift your perspective from narrow to complete. This means refocusing from the small picture (daily chores, daily irritations, closed-off emotions, or narrow views) to the big picture (deep connections with other people, your role in the world, emotional openness, or broad views). When we operate from a narrow perspective, we feel fearful and defensive, closed-off to anything that might hurt us. When we operate from a broad perspective, we feel calm and free, open to anything that life may bring.

Narrow Perspective	Broad Perspective
Daily tasks	Life goals
Irritations and resentments	Deep connections with others
Getting through the day	A sense of purpose
Needy	Centered
Anxious	Calm
Emotionally closed	Emotionally open
Self-centered	Part of a greater whole

Of course, there is a time and a place for both perspectives. No one can live in the big picture all the time. Even monks have to wash the dishes. That's how mindfulness practices were developed in the first place. When Buddhist monks had to take a break from meditation to do necessary chores, they tried to stay in the meditative mindset by focusing intently on what they were doing. It might seem like a paradox, but just paying attention to the present moment is often all it takes to switch your perspective to the big picture.

Eight Habits to Cultivate

Here are some mindful relationship habits you can start cultivating right away:

1. Practice, loving-kindness.

2. Own your feelings with "I" statements.

3. Find out what makes your partner feel loved.

4. Practice daily acts of love.

5. Tell your partner what you need.

6. Take care of yourself.

7. Disconnect from digital devices.

8. Be open to vulnerability.

Practice Loving Kindness

The mindful way to begin any conversation is with loving-kindness. This doesn't mean you can never raise any issues with your partner or that you must avoid conflict at all costs. Loving-kindness isn't fake and doesn't require you to suppress your real emotions behind a plastered-on smile.

Own Your Feelings with "I" Statements

You may have heard about the benefits of using "I" statements rather than "you" statements. Even if you've heard it all before, the benefits are real. "I" statements take ownership over your feelings rather than projecting them onto your partner. They are much less likely to make your partner feel criticized or attacked, so they are much less likely to trigger an adverse reaction.

Using "I" statements instead of "you" statements is mindful and a form of mindfulness training in its own right. To develop the habit of using "I" statements, you'll have to slow down and think about everything you say to your partner before you say it.

The act of slowing down and paying close attention is the basis of every mindfulness exercise, so you can improve your ability to be mindful just by making a conscious effort to develop this habit.

Find Out What Makes Your Partner Feel Loved

People don't all express love in the same way because people don't all want to receive love in the same way.

When both partners are giving the type of love they yearn to receive, they'll both feel unloved unless they happen to yearn for the same thing.

It's like they're speaking different languages.

According to Marriage Counselor Gary Chapman, most People Fit into one of five "Love Languages":

- **Words:** The use of loving words such as compliments, supportive statements, or romantic expressions.

- **Time:** Spending time fully engaged with each other without distractions of any kind. This can be as simple as playing a board game together or going for a walk, as long as your attention is entirely on your partner.

- **Presents:** Giving and receiving gifts such as jewelry, flowers, chocolate, journals — anything the other person will enjoy receiving

- **Service:** Doing things for the other person, like getting a glass of water or running an errand

- **Touch:** This can be anything from a hug to sexual intimacy. Some people are more focused on cuddling and physical closeness, and some are more focused on sexual touch, but either way, the physical connection is central.

The easiest way to find out what makes your partner feel loved is just to ask, but if your communication has broken down, this may not be so easy. If your partner isn't in touch with their feelings, they might not even be able to articulate what they need.

Practice daily Acts of Love

Once you know which love language your partner responds to. You can work that language into your daily life. For example, you could set aside a little time every day to give your partner your undivided personal attention, or you could take one errand or chore off their hands every day. You could make a point of coming home with flowers or other little gifts. You could make sure to hug them often and warmly.

Tell Your Partner What You Need

Expecting other people to be mind-readers is rarely effective and usually results in bitterness and resentment on both sides. Remember, your partner is probably trying to tell you how they feel even if you can't hear them — it's just that they're speaking in their love language rather than yours.

For example, perhaps you feel unloved because your partner is always giving you gifts you don't even want but never gets you a glass of water or carries something massive for you. Your partner is trying to speak the language of gifts when the language you understand best is service acts.

Remember to talk about your feelings, not their actions. "I love being held and need more cuddle time" has a good chance of being heard, but "you never want to cuddle with me" does not.

Take Care of Yourself

When you rely on your partner to provide everything you need in life, you put far too much weight on the relationship, and it inevitably suffers under strain. Of course, you want your partner to add something extraordinary to your life that wouldn't otherwise be there, but that doesn't mean they can meet every unresolved need you've ever had. No one can make you "feel whole" if you don't feel whole already.

Disconnect from Digital Devices

Everyone knows that digital devices are convenient, entertaining — and frequently distracting. If they weren't so good at claiming your attention, you wouldn't use them in the first place. Unfortunately, these devices have become so effective at claiming our attention that they alienate us from the people we love the most.

One of the best things you can do for your relationship is to give it your full attention and emotional engagement whenever possible.

This means disconnecting from digital devices when you're spending time together. Many people find it helpful to try to follow these rules:

- No device is used when you're having dinner together.
- No device is used when you're on a date together.
- Scheduled "no device" time whenever you both have the day off. You may not be able to shut the device off all day, but you should schedule as much device-free time as possible.
- Do things outside like going for a walk together, and don't bring your devices with you.
- Whenever possible, talk in person rather than send text messages.

Digital devices continually pull you away from the present moment. Every time you hear the alert and check your smartphone to see who texted you, your attention is drawn away from whatever you're doing at that moment. Digital devices always encourage you not to be mindful, and disconnecting from them will make it much easier to stay focused on your relationship.

Be Open to Vulnerability

This means two things at once: be open to your partner's vulnerability, and be open to your own. Vulnerability and intimacy go hand in hand. If you don't trust someone enough to show them who you are, how close are you ever likely to be? Vulnerability feels dangerous because someone who knows your inner weaknesses can take advantage of that information and do you serious harm. That's why it isn't usually a good idea to jump into an intimate relationship too quickly. Sharing vulnerabilities or asking you to do so too quickly is a red flag. Someone who does this might be a potential abuser trying to get a hook into you.

CHAPTER 3:

Prioritize Your Relationship with Meetings

Most of us would say we put our relationship first, but do we do that? Do we frequently offer priority to our relationship and our spouse or partner before jobs, digital devices, personal interests, and others?

Are we willing to sacrifice our time, resources, and emotional comfort to make sure we don't risk the intimacy, confidence, respect, and affection we share with our partner?

This is not a meeting to discuss your children, your lists of tasks, or your upcoming holiday. It's just a meeting to reflect on your relationship and discuss ways to make it stronger and healthier, and it should be the first habit that you set up together.

How Do You Grow this Habit?

If you're going through a severe struggle or dispute, you can meet every day until you feel like things are back on track and you've resolved. Otherwise, try to meet once a week or twice a month.

Discuss a Day and a Time of Day that Fits well for both of You

Choose a time when infants, jobs, or other life demands are less likely to be disrupted. Often, think of a moment when you're not under stress or pressure. It's probably not a good time until you leave for work in the morning. It would be easier to have a Sunday morning or an evening after the children are in bed.

Set Up a Series of Reminders or Prompts for a Meeting

This is particularly relevant if you only meet once a week or twice a week. The only tool that Steve suggests is Google Calendar. He and his wife use this method to share their schedule, including meetings, appointments, and upcoming activities related to their son. This makes it relatively easy for both of them to know precisely what the other person is doing at any point in the day. Only focus on your one habit for the first week to get the hang of it. Your following meeting to review your progress might not take too long, but you will appreciate your efforts' early success.

Please Take Notes in the Journal during the Conference

Both of you should take notes during your meetings to keep track of your success. This helps you see how your relationship and intimacy are changing and see what you need to continue working on.

During the meetings, you should write down suggestions, questions, or issues that you would like to discuss at the following meeting.

Set the Mood of the Conference

Try not to participate in debates or uncomfortable conversations before the conference, but not add negative energy. If you are too upset to have a constructive conversation, postpone your meeting until you are calmer.

Choose a meeting place conducive to a private, fruitful, respectful dialogue in which all partners feel equal. Delete any obstacles, such as computers and phones. Make sure that everyone else in the house knows not to disturb you.

Have a Meeting Agenda

Your discussions would be much more efficient if you decide what you want to do — whether separately or on both sides.

If you're working on a new habit of strengthening your relationship, explore this habit after talking about good things. Take turns expressing how well you think you've done with this new behavior and how well you think your partner has done.

Neither of you must attempt to mitigate your partner's feelings by justifying or deflecting your actions or denying that your partner's feelings are justified. Your joking remark may have been innocent, but your partner's feelings should be your priority.

Please Mind Your Job for the Coming Week

Based on what you mentioned at the meeting and the work you both need to do; discuss the steps you plan to take throughout the week to progress. Write it down in your diaries to remember the following week. Then end the meeting the same way you started it — with a hug, a kiss, and words of affirmation.

CHAPTER 4:

Lead with Respect and Kindness

B eing kind is one of the best things you can do to mend your relationship. When you aren't getting along with your partner, passions are flying in the wrong way. Both of you want to be right, want to state your points. A lot of kindness can be lost in these moments because you likely feel frustrated and exhausted by the relationship's dynamic. All couples' fight; it is inevitable. What matters is how you are communicating during your disagreements and what you do after they are over. Those who continually "make up" without making any changes will only find themselves in the same situation again in the future. If you know that you are in a bad mood or angry with your partner, do not jump into an in-depth discussion. You need to take some time for yourself to calm down and collect your thoughts. The things you say out of anger are often the most regrettable, so your aim should be to avoid this at all costs. If something is becoming too much for you, ask for a little alone time to gather yourself. Take some deep breaths to empty your mind and find your center. Once you feel that you are calming down, get to the root of your facing. Figure out what is causing you to feel gloomy and why. You won't always have clear answers, but calming yourself down before you talk to your partner will automatically result in a better outlook for the two of you.

Couples need hobbies of their own, space to exist outside of the relationship. When you spend too much time together, there is a higher chance you will become frustrated with one another. This is when kindness is forgotten. If you just feel that you cannot get along, you might need to spend some time doing things that you individually enjoy. Plus, distance makes the heart grow fonder. When you are away from your partner, either hanging out with friends or engaging in a personal hobby, you will begin to miss certain aspects of being with them. Taking some time to do activities apart does not mean your relationship has to suffer. It can be one of the healthiest decisions you make as a couple.

Your partner is the closest person to you. Because you know each other so well, you also know that the love you have for each other is unconditional. For this reason, it becomes easy to take your anger out on your partner subconsciously. Even if they haven't done anything wrong, projecting your frustrations onto them might feel okay because you know they will forgive you. This doesn't mean it is fair, though. When you are feeling down, make sure you take full accountability for why this is happening. Do not place this burden on your partner. If you need to talk about the issue, you can vent to your partner, but do not misdirect any of your anger toward them. This will only create a combative situation where kindness will go out the window.

In any situation, you can likely feel when things are getting tense. If the tension rises too much, you will slip up and say something you don't mean. Part of anger management is avoiding these situations before they blow up. If you are in a heated discussion with your partner, you cannot calm down and vocalize that you need some time to think. If they do the same to you, respect their wishes. This will allow the situation to settle down and give you both the chance to think before you speak. So many people who run their mouths end up feeling regret and guilt once everything has been said. You don't want to be left with these feelings.

Think about why you first started dating your partner, what you love most about them. Getting back to your roots can bring up a renewed feeling of kindness. Do some of the things that you used to do for them before you two were official. These courting gestures usually disappear once you make things official, but they do not have to. The same goes for flirting — continue to flirt with your partner, even if you have been together for a while! It is very kind of you to think about your partner's enjoyment and how you can bring more of this into their life. Try to do nice things for them always, not just on special occasions. Your actions will speak volumes.

Kindness also builds trust. If your partner knows that you can respond kindly to anything, they will feel safe telling you everything. Those with explosive tempers often push their partners away or become abusive because they cannot get over their own internalized insecurities. Being open-minded and kind is the way to go. You should want your partner to feel comfortable telling you anything, even if it is unpleasant. That is the beauty of honesty and healthy communication. If your temper has been wrong in the past, it is not too late to change this. Make bold choices that will show your partner that you want them to feel safe and comfortable.

CHAPTER 5:

Cherish Your Partner

If they repeat the mistake or do something similar, then your understanding and hope begin to head from the window. After that, your partner is frequently reminded of the inability to keep their word, and they're judged according to what happened. The relationship changes and the guilty partner might find him/herself reluctant to invest in it, as the outcomes aren't always positive.

When you stop allowing your partner to redeem themselves, then you've undoubtedly also stopped believing in him/her. Whatever they may tell you, a little voice in your head will start reminding you that you should not trust them. Then, before you realize what happened, there will be frustration, discord, and pain in your relationship.

That's the point where you start to become suspicious, and your ideas can negatively influence your activities. Sometimes you might believe that your partner did something, even if you've got zero proof to back up your idea; many of the things they say seem to be a lie.

Jealousy stems from a lack of confidence and fear, and it induces insecurity and nervousness in the relationship.

Whenever you're jealous, insecure, and nervous, you're permanently on the watch for unproven lies or inconsistencies out of your partner. You patiently wait for them to slide up, proving that your concerns were set. Your feelings are rooted in fear, and even though you attempt to find proof to back up your ideas, you do it with your heart continuously racing because of hope.

Taking Charge of Your Emotions on Your Relationship

The very first step to take care of your jealousy is to understand and admit that you're doubtful of your partner. Being aware of it will block you from blaming them for your feelings and helping them do something to solve the issue. Once you admit your emotions, you enable yourself to fix your relationship. From the moment you understand that you're making a conscious choice in being jealous, you can discharge that anxiety and opt to trust your loved one. You may start by looking at your partner with a new pair of eyes, looking at what he/she does with a positive and proactive attitude, instead of a cynical and negative one. This suggestion isn't quite as simple as it might sound, but it may be accomplished.

This usually means that you decide to leave the past in the past and 'judge' your partner's actions starting today. It's hard, but living the present can be quite liberating; not having any negative feelings or background concerns lets you trust your partner better when telling you something.

You won't prejudge their behavior, and you won't wind up unhappy painful memories. When your partner calls to let you know they'll be working late, assure him/her that it's okay and hang up the telephone; don't start asking a lot of questions like where are you? Who are you with? What are you doing? Why are you doing that to me?

Instead, you might ask questions like if they're okay, have they had something to eat, or would they enjoy a hot bath when they get home. This attitude will probably not place your partner in a defensive mood; actually, he/she might start rushing to complete everything sooner, so they could come home to a loving setting. After the telephone call, rather than sitting and imagining your partner with another individual, envision them doing exactly what they told you they were about to do. So, when they get home, they're most likely to come across a more relaxed you, seeking to help them get a load of stress off their shoulders. Keep in mind that if they break your confidence and they lie to you, they are not making a fool out of you. They are making a fool out of themselves. In cases like this, they're the ones harming the relationship, and you'd be justified in choosing to leave. You aren't accountable for their behavior. You're only for your own, such as the way you respond to the situations. Trust is the basis of any relationship.

Strategies for Trusting on Your Partner

\

What both of you have to do is to find out how to trust each other. One of the best ways to start doing it is to believe on your own. In reality, trusting yourself is the first thing that anyone must consider when seeking to address any sort of trust issues, and that makes sense since if you do not trust yourself, you're never likely to trust someone else.

If it comes to trust your loved one, you will have to have a critical look at yourself, and no, we aren't talking about believing in yourself. All you have to know when it comes to trust problems is that they often turn into an issue because you're struggling with some type of questions. For example, if you're concerned about your partner cheating on you, it might be associated with you having ideas about cheating them.

Trust-Building Exercises

Trust-building exercises may help to build it back again, but they may also be used to earn a fantastic and healthier relationship. If you're all set to focus on fixing these problems, below are a few very efficient exercises you should try.

Fall Back

Probably this is the most known one, as everyone has heard about it, but also the most difficult one to execute, even if you fully trust your partner. This exercise requires that you stand facing your spouse and just let yourself fall back, expecting them to grab you.

CHAPTER 6:

Touch Often

Touch was the first form of communication we understood as infants. Therefore, it can affect us in a much deeper way than mere words. As adults, we develop filters and defenses that help protect us from being affected by words. Nowadays, we are bombarded by so many advertisements that we learn to diminish the impact of almost everything we hear. Yet, touch is different. We tend to think that a person's touch is very "honest," whereas their words are subject to question. A loving touch can slide past a person's defenses and touch them at their core if you want to know how to powerfully and efficiently give your partner the three you need to learn how to touch your mate lovingly.

Loving touch is entirely different than a sexual touch. Some people confuse the two, and they end up paying a high price. Sexual touching is excellent, but it doesn't replace what a nonsexual touch can do. Many of my female clients complain that their partner never touches them unless they want to have sex. When this occurs, women typically interpret this behavior as the man saying, "I don't really like you, but I'm willing to have sex with you to satisfy my own selfish needs." It's no wonder that their partner's touch does not arouse women in such situations. Yet, when men frequently touch their partners in a caring, nonsexual manner, the women feel safe and loved. When a woman feels truly safe and loved, she becomes much more interested in sex than when she feels she is being used.

Men and women are different when it comes to their sexual and emotional needs. In a recent study, 70 percent of all women said they would gladly never have sexual intercourse again as long as they were able to cuddle or have a long hug each day with their partner. I advise my counseling clients to find out their partner's precise touching needs and satisfy them as best they can. Although there are a few exceptions, the basic rule in relationships is the more you satisfy your partner's needs, the more they will want to satisfy your needs. I encourage couples to communicate about the precise forms of touch them most and least desirable. We tend to assume that other people are like us, which just isn't true. As you and your partner regularly touch each other in enjoyable ways, the amount of intimacy in your relationship will skyrocket.

Laurie and Jeff came to my office, complaining of a lack of passion in their relationship. They were both successful career people, highly intelligent, and very friendly with each other. They even communicated pretty well and were adept at avoiding blame or arguments. Everything was in good working order from the neck up, but there was no energy from the neck down. They would have sex about twice a month, but it lacked passion. They came to me wondering what, if anything, was wrong. I asked them how much they touch each other throughout the day. They each gave me a look like, "What does that have to do with anything?" From the expressions on their faces, I knew I had hit pay dirt. Their minds were being massaged with friendly words and good conversation, but their hearts, bodies, and souls were being ignored.

They took the prescribed medicine. A week after, they were physically all over each other in our counseling session, whereas before, they had been on opposite sides of the couch. If I hadn't been there forcing them to be civilized, I think they would have made love right there in my office! Nonsexual touch regularly can be strong love medicine.

CHAPTER 7:

Create Shared Rituals

Exploration proposes that couples who are fun-loving together have closer and more fulfilling relationships.

Shockingly, we people will, in general, become less perky as we get more seasoned. Play requires a touch of opportunity and space; by definition, it is anything but a profitable action. Life schedules and worries can infringe on our relationship and drain the fun-loving nature out of it.

Why Is Trouble Being Fun-Loving?

Why are people fun-loving? That probably won't be a question you've at any point posed to yourself. However, it's one that consumes the psyches of developmental scholars, even though (at least on its surface) play doesn't appear to add to our endurance. As opposed to investing the time chasing for food or resting to set aside energy, why would it be valuable for our progenitors to stay nearby the fire doing amusing impersonations of one another? Wouldn't that divert them from potential dangers that may be crawling out of the shrubs?

Playfulness, a few scientists guess, could fill in as a sign to expected mates. Men who take part in a benevolent, corresponding play with others may be exhibiting their absence of hostility — an attractive characteristic when savage guys are a danger to their spouses and kids — and ladies who have the energy for play may be showing their energy, an intermediary for their conceptive capacities. At least that is how individual analysts decipher the finding that, as per studies, individuals appear to search for playfulness, humor, and a carefree demeanor in possible partners.

What Does romantic Play Resemble?

We can take numerous energetic ways toward intimacy — and there's something we can gain from how analysts have listed, sorted, and accounted for all the various ways partners play.

One of the most widely recognized types of play is by all accounts the mystery language that creates between couples, from monikers to private jokes.

The pretense is likewise standard. In the solace of the romantic bubble, one may have a sense of security enough to claim to be a little dog, make their best Elvis impression, or mirror the neighbor's strangely piercing snicker.

Some play requires no words by any means — my partner's moving being one model. We can energetically steal a treat from our cherished, transforming a typically childish act into a warm trade. Prodding is another behavior that pushes it among positive and negative, so play is a fragile exchange: Our partner needs to see our perky aim and participate in the game if they are irritated by our silliness put off by our come emotionally pokes.

Some play is more organized, similar to the guidelines and games that couples create. When I'm discussing Fred over a Google-able purpose of actuality, we frequently wager three kisses on the appropriate response before finding it — and the washout needs to pay their obligation promptly.

In these manners, play appears to emerge precipitously. In any case, then those erratic remarks or practices transform into propensities, transforming and advancing after some time yet continually communicating a first love and comprehension.

In this way, it most likely shocks no one that lively couples are frequently cheerful couples. In considers that recall individuals about their practices and feelings, the individuals who are perkier in their relationships will, in general, experience increased positive emotions, be happier with their relationship, and feel closer to one another. They report that they convey better, resolve clashes better, and see their links positively.

What Sort of Play Will Work for You?

When we think about our relationships, those fun-loving minutes are things to esteem. In the ordinary, two individuals energetically develop a mystery language and culture in the ordinary's daily schedule, and it is exclusively their own. Play includes demonstrating our partner parts of ourselves that others once in a while observe, the uncorrupt, senseless side that probably won't be socially adequate at work or in different settings. Playing is inspecting the obscure outskirts of two minds, whose forms can turn out to be reassuringly natural just through the experience of shared weakness and nonjudgmental responsiveness. It is through playing that we figure out how to move toward somebody's more cozy self.

Consequently, there's nobody a size-fits-all approach to play with your partner. Each couple's play will look somewhat changed, and that is the point. If there were any solution, it would be something like this: Let your senseless self-come out, value the silliness of your cherished one, and do what makes you both grins.

CHAPTER 8:

Develop Active Listening

If you want to build healthy communication skills, listening is essential. It will only help you build a long-lasting, happy relationship. When you feel you are being heard, you feel empowered. It will give you a boost to share even more because other people will show they care.

They'll acknowledge what you say and validate you. You need to do the same to validate your partner. Listening must go both ways; there can't be only one side listening. This will make one of you feel unappreciated and will disconnect you. The relationship will suffer. Before we learn how to listen, let's look at the reasons why we don't listen. It could be because of distractions or the inability to focus. We all experience these barriers, and we need to overcome them to learn active listening.

There are different types of blocks we encounter when we should be carefully listening. They are easy to overcome with some extra focus, but you won't notice if you don't become aware of them. So, let's list some.

1. **Comparing:** This usually happens when we listen to our partner talk, but we continuously compare

his experience with our own. This block is familiar with people who have insecurities.

2. **Mind reading:** It happens when the one who listens tries to predict what the speaker will say after or tries to figure out what the speaker means or feels.

3. **Rehearsing:** This happens when the one who is supposed to be listening is obsessed with what he will respond to the speaker, or if he is following to talk.

4. **Filtering:** If we find a particular subject unpleasant, we can often catch our mind wandering and not be prepared to listen to the unpleasant story.

5. **Dreaming:** Simply put, the listener is daydreaming and not paying attention to the speaker.

6. **Identifying:** The listener often interrupts the speaker to share his experience with a particular subject.

7. **Advising:** The listener interrupts the speaker with the advice he or she has to offer even before the speaker is done with his story.

8. **Sparring:** This happens when the listener is interrupting the speaker to disagree or to debate.

9. **Being right:** This happens when the listener does not allow the speaker to prove him wrong.

10. **Derailing:** The listener, for one reason or another, changes the subject.

11. **Placating:** The listener is more focused on being supportive and sounding pleasant than listening.

We all have listening blocks, some of which we are aware of, and some aren't. Listening blocks are the bad habits that will hold our relationship back. We need to get rid of these bad habits if we want to build a healthy, long-lasting relationship. Which of the listening blocks listed above do you recognize in yourself? It can be more than one depending on the situation and the person who is speaking. Think of your partner. You probably know what in his tone triggers one of these listening blocks. For a happy relationship, it is of great importance to be open but not just about yourself. You also need to be open about the things your partner is telling you.

Learn active Listening

Now that you are aware of your listening blocks, you must engage the conversation process and listen to your partner. Active listening means you can respond to your partner's stories, not just with words but with body language and facial expressions. This will not only tell your reactions; it will also indicate that you are genuinely listening. As a person with relationship insecurities, there are things available for you to help you not just be a better listener but to learn more about your insecurities, and you will see them clearly for what they are:

- **Paraphrasing:** When dealing with insecurities, it is essential to paraphrase what your partner is saying. This will leave no space for miscommunication, and you will know what your partner is communicating. Paraphrasing is useful for remembering conversations, and if you bring it up, there will be no misunderstandings.

- **Clarifying:** It is more an extension of paraphrasing, but it means you will ask questions to make sure you understand your partner. You will get more information by doing so, and you will be able to fill any gaps you had in understanding. It will also let your partner know you are actively communicating with him or her.

- **Feedback:** Simply respond to your partner's story. You can even talk about how their story influenced you and how it made you feel. Giving feedback is an excellent opportunity to open up and be honest with your partner. But be sure to ask your partner how he feels about his story. You might have an understanding of his thoughts, but you are still uncertain of how he feels. Don't shy away from asking questions when you are giving feedback.

CHAPTER 9:

Manage Your Anger

Anger partly makes inroads into interpersonal relationships, and in specific ways and sizes that come in, we don't always identify as anger. There's the screaming, aggressive version that most of us think about when we hear someone get angry — the kind of anger that depletes. Some of us don't like being around people who are outwardly and aggressively angry, and some of us react in ways that are incredibly unhelpful and even detrimental to us.

And there is anger which doesn't feel like anger at all. Imagine I'm mad because you didn't turn up for a lunch date on time.

Rather than calmly telling you how I feel (confused and irritated), I feel nothing is wrong. If you're trying to talk with me, I'm listening to you barely and minimally, making you make all the effort.

Soon you would be able to say, "What's the matter?" I'm saying, "What are you talking about? There's nothing wrong with that!" If not noisy and offensive, passive-aggression is dangerous in its unique way.

Understanding the Impact of Anger on Your Relationship

Do you live with a partner's wrath, which has become a constant source of discomfort to you? Do you now feel like your whole life is designed to stop, deter, or monitor your partner's anger? And do you think that your partner's anger is a vortex that pulls you in, drives you to join in the outrage, and contributes to an endless series of wars, combat battles, and scorekeeping? Many of the other couples follow each other's lead, and their routines seem unchanging. Disharmonious speech by one partner sets the stage for the other. In these unacceptable displays of frustration, all these people have been lost; no one can clarify what needs to be said or settle problems that cook under the surface. It's only standard that you become angry in reaction to what you believe is an unjust hostility directed towards you. It's only fair that your partner takes responsibility for changing the drill when it feels like your partner's anger is pulling the rug from under you. Exactly right?

How We Get Entangled

If you're in a well-established and loving relationship with this person, it makes sense to want them to be encouraged to make some changes. How do you keep the rush because your partner doesn't seem to have it?

What Options Do You Have?

If the relationship stays the way it is and you continue to live unhappily with this person, when is the time to say "enough?" Proposing to leave a committed relationship may be easy for someone else, particularly when children and other shared responsibilities tie you together, but it's never an easy option. As we'll be addressing, setting firm boundaries on what's reasonable and what you're reluctant to consider is critical to deciding to leave. You will leave immediately if your safety or that of other family members is in jeopardy. First, we're going to explore the real possibilities that you can, directly and indirectly, influence what's happening to this person after so you don't have to plan an escape.

To address these problems, you need to know more about the dynamics of the relationships: what you do will influence what the other person thinks and feels, and then decide to do so. The reverse is also real — what your partner immediately impacts on you and can set the stage for you to make changes you never thought you'd be making.

The Nature of Change in Relationships

How are you changing someone when that person hasn't wanted to do it on their own and can't even believe there's a problem there?

Let's look at what you can personally handle, and at the disadvantages of your strength. I'm not going to suggest that I can control any other living thing.

Seek to "make" a polite adolescent all the time, or a three-year-old live in the backyard, without building a fence, if you don't believe me. We'll be seeking help from others. We will praise and thank them if they impress us, and even reject or punish them in some way if they fail to meet our expectations. And we limit ourselves to persuasion and feedback — not to control. And this also extends to the situations in which we love others to carry out their angry feelings.

There's one silver lining, though. And if we can't guilt-trip or threaten enough to get others to stop the bad things they're doing, we're mostly liable for what we're doing in response or proactively handling living with a wrathful person. When recalling what you are doing now when your loved one is unreasonably angry or lonely, you will also be determining how effective the solution has been and taking steps to strengthen it.

Learning a new Pattern

It's not easy to break free from a routine you're used to, even though you know you've been trapped. Psychologist Harriet Lerner describes the interdependent behaviors of a couple as a "dance." Each one has "steps" that impact on what the other is doing. Behavioral habits can get so unconscious that we engage in them without fully aware of what we're doing. So, in general, the first step is to become conscious, when upset, of exactly how we respond to a loved one's "dance movements." If you don't like the new "dance," the steps may shift, and your partner may or may not follow your lead-but the old "dance of rage" is over.

CHAPTER 10:

Reduce The Use of Social Media and digital Devices

Innovation is inevitable in the contemporary globe. A couple of work continues to be that they do not need a daily computer system; social media sites have linked people worldwide. The internet has also become the go-to resource of details. Facebook has, somehow, replaced the night news as people's means of learning more about worldwide and national events. Instagram and also YouTube have developed an entirely brand-new breed of celeb. In contrast, the easy availability of photo editing and enhancing software has permitted a generation of models to look impossibly remarkable on paper. The globe has become wired, and with the arrival of smart devices, and most individuals are linked to the digital earth from the moment they get up in the early morning.

Considerable innovation use has been linked to stress and anxiety, sleeplessness, anxiety, and depression. Also, a few of the electronic age's most positive attributes are the reason for these significant troubles. The web contains info in any way times, from practical realities about damaging news or identifying a cardiovascular disease to baffling triviality such as how many bananas a person would certainly have to consume to struggle with potassium poisoning and also warmed debates about the length of time it would undoubtedly consider zombies to overwhelm significant cities.

Living bordered by this deluge of information triggers information overload. The brain has a hard time sorting with the consistent flow of details, and also, a person starts to stay in a state of subconscious anxiety and stress. This is because the brain is hardwired to filter information, mainly aesthetic details such as the photos and text that make up most of the material on the internet. This uncontrollable and subconscious examination is a holdover transformative trait from when stopping working from evaluating aesthetic information appropriately could cause a person to get eaten by a starving lion.

The brain, nevertheless, is an astonishingly adaptable body organ. Eventually, it finds out to more or less stay on par with the constant flow of info. It discovers to expect the overwhelming influx of new data, and also being able to manufacture even more details is much better, right? Wrong. The mind sheds the capability to focus on something for an extended period because it is regularly expecting brand-new excitement. This is called "uniqueness addiction," or, more informally, "snacks brain." Smartphones only aggravate this neurological overstimulation since the web goes to a person's fingertips whatsoever times.

Heavy mobile phone usage can result in smartphone dependency, a subset of net addiction. Many individuals experience this condition that it has all but come to be the standard in society. Think of it, the number of people find it strange when a pal is twitchy throughout the day because they forgot their phone in your home? Do individuals act shocked if the pal's initial response to getting their phone back is to scroll hysterically via their texts, emails, as well as social media, feeds to see what they missed out on? The odd or impolite person is the one that tells their meant conversation partner to do away with their mobile phone until both are done speaking.

This obsession with smartphones likewise puts social media at an individual's fingertips, and also social networks itself is the source of numerous troubles. Possibly one of the most overlooked concerns with social media sites is the effect it has on rest. Hundreds of people keep up late during the night, scrolling through Facebook or switching breaks on Snapchat. This late-night social media scrolling results in countless people skipping out on slumber both due to bedtime and because the blue light from electronic screens reduces melatonin production. Such social media sites-based insomnia is an even more severe issue for teenagers that make up a substantial percentage of today's social media site users because teens need even more rest than adults.

Social media site likewise leads to stress and anxiety, envy, as well as clinical depression. People put their lives on social media sites and unconsciously obsess over how many likes their blog posts obtain. Considering that social media sites allow people to portray themselves as a particular method, most people only see the very best items of their Facebook good friends' lives. This leads to coveting, resentment, and also misery with their own life. Continuous contact with the online world likewise opens the doors for cyberbullying. This form of intimidation can be a lot more ferocious and destructive than in-person bullying since the bully can hide behind their keyboard's anonymity. There is no way, in most cases, for the sufferer to eliminate back. In acute situations, some teens have been cyberbullied so terribly that they have ended up being self-destructive.

Social media sites' adverse results on genuine relationships have brought about a generation of teens and kids that feel separated and lonesome. The social network does not just disrupt the right relations.

There is a large amount of excellent that can appear in technology, but it has a dark side that many people cheerfully disregard. Offered the rising prices of teen self-destruction and enhancing grievances about university graduates who cannot hold a typical discussion, it is time that individuals attend to the very genuine threats of the electronic age. They require to assess precisely how technology usage is connected to anxiety and choose what kind of interpersonal abilities they want their youngsters to have when they grow up. However, people need first to utilize their mind to do what it was indicated to do. They need to stop seeking to Lord Google and Woman iPhone for answers and also believe.

CHAPTER 11:

Learn to Love Yourself

Can you tell me frankly you love yourself? Have you had a hard time being comfortable with yourself? Focusing on your shortcomings is too simple that everyone will focus on their insecurities rather than on the things about themselves they're pleased with. Doing this will make you hate yourself. You can also be too distracted to concentrate on those around you and not concentrate on enjoying yourself. Some people don't want to be isolated, so they are afraid to do anything themselves. It will also delay your self-love path because you have to learn to be confident with yourself. So, keep reading and figure out how to treat one another today. And, we'll take a look at specific ways you can fall in love with yourself and help you get going on your path towards self-esteem. Let's first remember that you deserve to respect yourself.

Why Is It So important to Love Yourself?

Some might think this more important than others, but self-love is one of the best things you can do for yourself.

Falling in love with yourself gives you faith, self-esteem, and can simply make you more optimistic.

You may also note that falling in love is better for you because you have first learned to love yourself.

Facts about Self Love in Relationships

1. **People Treat You the Way They See You Treat Yourself**

   If you handle yourself with no respect or affection, you are effectively encouraging someone to do the same. Place yourself high expectations, then. Be willing to get up and say, "I am stronger than this. I won't tolerate that happening to me. "If you don't love yourself first, you won't have any standard of how others should treat you. It's much harder to understand that you have pure self-love that people give you less than you deserve.

2. **You Can't Depend on other People to Make You Feel Loved**

   It can lead to dysfunctional relationships not only with others but with yourself, relying on other people to make you feel special. If you don't have a romantic relationship with yourself, you will still not represent love in your relationships with others. At least not in the way you could when you first knew yourself. It is the same idea as to when we're talking about self-care, "you can't drink from an empty cup." Visualize filling yourself with inside out passion. Unlike the outside in that will depend on other people to make you feel safe. Fill yourself with so much passion that it is pouring out of your relationships with others.

3. **A Relationship Should Be a Relationship, Not a codependent Situation**

It comes back to the argument of not making you feel loved or deserving of relying on other men. Codependency is described as "excessive emotional or psychological reliance on a partner, usually a partner who needs help due to sickness or addiction." Typically, this dysfunctional relationship can grow if both spouses severely lose self-love, self-confidence, self-worth, etc.

There are different rates of this, but it's not a safe condition, regardless.

4. **No One Can Make You happy the Way You Can Make Yourself happy**

That is real! I think who knows you better than you do?

Learn how to make yourself happy to communicate how they can make you happy to future partners.

Anyway, if your relationship with yourself isn't yet there, you can end up ruining a perfectly good relationship. If you don't know how to be happy and just derive joy from your relationship, you place a lot of pressure on your partner to keep you happy always. Such pressure is unfair and can end up damaging the whole relationship.

How to Love Yourself?

Here are only 15 ideas that you should use and figure out how to enjoy yourself and get your confidence today!

1. Have Fun by Yourself

It's always nice to schedule for yourself a couple of days, that's just for you to do something fun. You can learn to enjoy your own business by doing so, and most definitely become more comfortable about doing so on your own.

2. Travel Once a Year

It may be out of the comfort zone altogether, but that is a positive thing! If you can fly alone, this would be an excellent taste of self-love. You're going to discover new things not only about yourself but also about a different world. It makes you get out of your daily schedule, too.

3. Start a Journal

If you can write down your ideas and emotions, so any time, you can look out and see how you coped in those circumstances.

4. Give Yourself a Break

We may often be harsh on ourselves, that's normal, but you have to allow yourself a break from time to time.

5. Make a List of Your Accomplishments

Creating a list of what you've accomplished is a great way to fall in love. That makes you feel good about yourself, and from what you have accomplished, find happiness. Sometimes we can focus on the negatives and forget about the positives, so this is a great way to remember what you've achieved.

6. Pursue new Interests

Trying something different that you wanted to do for a while or too afraid to do is perfect. Until you try it, you never know what you might enjoy, so think of a new hobby you could try, or go to a place you wanted to go to for some time.

7. Give Yourself Credit Where Credit Is Due

Feast on your successes! Much as when you mention your successes, celebrating your milestones is nice too. Tell us what you did, share your stories, and be proud of what you did. Give yourself that credit that you deserve.

8. Work on Your Self-Trust

A perfect way to display self-love is to have faith in yourself and your intuition. You will most likely know what's best for you, and self-confidence is a step toward self-love.

9. **Take Care of Yourself**

Perhaps this one is trivial, but taking care of yourself plays a huge role in learning how to love yourself when others do not. When you're looking after yourself, you'll be the best version of yourself. Look at our self-care suggestions to get you going.

CHAPTER 12:

Apologize More Often

One critical way to build trust, rekindle intimacy, and connect emotionally with your partner is to learn to apologize when you hurt them. In the long-life journey of love as a couple, there will be moments of arguments and broken promises, which will result in hurting each other's feelings. At such times, learning to say "sorry" can save your relationship. Learning to apologize to your partner is a crucial life and marriage skill. It is difficult to say sorry or apologizes to your partner, mostly if you belong to the class of individuals who view that as a sign of weakness.

When you understand what it means to you and your spouse, offering an apology becomes easier. Apologizing is one way to show that you are selfless and care for your partner's feelings. It shows that you are treating your partner the way you wish to be treated when you are hurt. It is a simple way to admit your faults, and that you are willing to correct yourself and try to do better after. It is a way to own up your mistakes by acknowledging that you are an imperfect human being, and you can be wrong sometimes. It shows that you are willing to make an effort to grow from your mistakes and become a better partner.

Admit Your Mistakes

The first essential step in learning to apologize to your husband or wife is to admit that you are a human being and are eligible for making a mistake. This makes it easier for you to accept that you have a problem, and you are wrong in one way or another. Unless you accept that you are wrong, your apology cannot be genuine, sincere, or meaningful. You will just say it for the sake of avoiding a further argument, and it may not reflect your actual position, attitude, or facial expression. So the first thing is learning to admit and accept your mistakes. Show that you are willing to be fully responsible for what you did and take the necessary corrective measures going forward.

Learn to Respect, the Emotions of Your Partner

When our partners do something wrong, we get hurt. Anyone who has been in a relationship knows this to be accurate, and it is a rule with no exceptions. All of us feel hurt when it happens. As you approach your partner for an apology, it is good to keep this in mind after doing something wrong. Show that it wasn't intentional and put yourself into your partner's shoes. This will show that you respect how they feel, and you will do your best to avoid making them feel the same after.

Be sincere with Your Apology

Listen to your partner as they vent out, and do not interfere until they have finished explaining how they feel. This will help you understand their perspective and the extent to which your actions have hurt them. That way, you will offer a sincere and honest apology reflecting your true feelings and attitude towards how they feel. Don't begin to explain why you did what you did or start to give excuses. This will be a sign that you don't care, because you will be trying to justify your deeds. Be as specific as possible in your apology and just focus on that one issue at hand, which your partner has raised.

Humble Yourself and Ask for Forgiveness

It shows how humble and caring you are to your spouse when you present yourself in person and offer a face-to-face apology. You may want to write a letter, send an email, or a text message, but that should come as a way to emphasize what you have already verbalized. If you find it hard to face your spouse and verbalize the apology, you need to dig deep and unearth what prevents you from doing the same. Don't be that kind of a spouse who gathers the courage to communicate face to face only when fighting. Master the courage to face your partner and offer an apology. After making an apology, take it one step further and ask your spouse to forgive you.

Forgive Yourself

To show compassion to your partner, you must be able to be compassionate with yourself first. To welcome and accept your partner's forgiveness, you must be ready to forgive yourself too. It may not be easy to forgive yourself, especially after realizing the severity of the extent of the emotional damage you have caused your partner. Forgiving yourself gives you the confidence to work on yourself and make critical changes to rise above your mistakes. Failure to forgive yourself can make you begin to play the victim. You may end up with inward resentment, which can make it hard for you to forgive or accept forgiveness from your spouse. This can limit your chances of becoming better.

Create an Action Plan

You don't want to keep on apologizing all the time for doing the same things. The best way to avoid the same issues from cropping up is to develop an action plan. You need to develop a list of things or steps you will follow to avoid repeating mistakes. It makes no sense to your partner when you keep repeating mistakes and apologizing every time you do so. If it was a communication mishap, focus on improving your communication skills. If it was a delayed payment of some bills, come up with a way to remind yourself of such responsibilities. You can set a reminder on your phone or the calendar.

Put Your Action Plan into Practice

Take bold steps to practice your action plan. No amount of rhetoric can take the place of what you do. As they say, action speaks louder than words. Let your actions reflect your commitment to making sure that the same issues don't arise again by acting your words. Change your behavior by putting the requisite effort to make up for your faults. This will eliminate any fears or doubts your spouse might have developed as a result of your mistakes. They will begin to rebuild their trust and intimacy once they see that you are putting a lot of effort into becoming better.

CHAPTER 13:

Spice Up Your Sex Life

Why does good sex fade even when couples love each other very much? Can we want what we already have? Why is forbidden so erotic? What is it about indiscretion that makes desire so potent? And why does sex make babies, but babies make way for erotic train-smashes between couples? When you love, how does it feel? And when you desire, how is that different? These are some of the questions that we face in modern love.

Talking about modern love, let's just refer back to how our modern (millennial) society is becoming increasingly individualistic. A big part of our relationships entails sex and sexual desires, so we need to look at how we approach it today and age.

Today, we still need to feel secure. We want predictability, dependability, reliability. We need anchoring experiences in our lives. A place to call home. But, in the same breath, we also don't want to feel stuck in a mundane routine. We have a kind of contradicting need, too — and it's an intense need. It is a need for adventure, novelty, mystery, risk, danger, the unexpected and mysterious. We want to travel and see things, but we also want a place to call home.

These kinds of options weren't readily available to most couples or marriages back in the day. Marriage used to be more of an economic institution in which people were given a partnership for life for social status, children, and companionship. Today, however, we still seek these "perks"— but besides, we want our partners to be our best friends, confidants, economic partners, and insatiable lovers. And on top of that, we live twice as long, so these wants and needs have to be maintained over a much more extended period.

We are expecting one person to give us what a whole community used to provide. We ask for belonging, identity, consistency, but also transcendence and mystery. We ask for comfort and edge. We ask for novelty and familiarity. We ask for predictability and surprise. No wonder we're so confused when it comes to relationships and sex. We are sitting with a crisis of desire.

Yet our crisis of desire is in our minds. And again, it all comes down to a mindful approach to our relationship. Even when it comes to sex, no, wait, especially when it comes to sex. Once we are aware that we are facing a crisis of desire, and that the crisis nestled itself into our minds and imaginations, we can do something about it.

Keep this in mind when you go into the bedroom. It doesn't matter if you're in a committed relationship and want to spice things up or if you're just starting out and still getting to know each other. Take a mindful moment to remind yourself (and even your partner) that your imagination lies at the heart of keeping the spark of desire ignited. Now, let's allow our imaginations to run wild for a while with some of the ideas below!

Dirty Weekend Getaway

I know we said mystery is not a place to go but instead looking through new eyes. Still, it doesn't mean that we have to completely discard the mystery and adventure you can experience by visiting a new destination. Some alone time away in an unknown place elevates the sexiness factor. Plus, if you reserve smartly, you don't even have to make the bed. Make a point to get jiggy at least once a day while you're away.

Play a Game

If playfulness is also one of the ingredients of "erotic intelligence," why not get into actually playing a game (or two). You could invest in some board games for couples, or just get the engines running with a round of strip poker. Or, set a timer so you can take turns choosing what to do after. If need be, invest in a set of sex dice to get you going. Play around with your partner to see what games work for you both.

Talk about Your Fantasies

Perhaps you have always wanted to do it in a pool. Maybe he wanted to do it on the beach. Or maybe one of you has been curious about a little role play. It's time to get the image inside your head out on the sheets for your partner to explore with you. If you can't play them out, you can always pretend. If you can't do it on the Great Wall of China, try acting like the long corner couch is the wall. This can go hand in hand with "playing games" or just keeping that playful, creative spirit alive.

Switch Things Up

Don't just always stick to the trusty old' featherbed. There are so many locations in the house, or even just within your room. You can try some new music or do it at a different time of the day. Keeping things as fresh and new as possible is vital. And then, of course, there are so many resources and ideas for some new positions that it might be great fun to search online where you and your partner can work through!

New Lingerie

New lingerie might not be the most mindful thing. Women underestimate the level of confidence some fancy lingerie can bring to the table. You can even take your partner along on the shopping trip. Men are visual creatures, and the anticipation will make them feel randy up until the grand reveal. Alternatively, just grab a few new items you feel confident in and surprise him when he gets home.

Be a little naughty

Get out of your comfort zone by trying a little dirty talk. Perhaps try a little spanking or make your partner wear a blindfold. Bring in a little tickle feather. Keep it playfully naughty.

Double the Foreplay

This one is for pleasing the ladies. Though men are visual creatures and go nuts in anticipation of some sexy time, women may need some more revving up. Touch her all over. Be gentle yet firm. Oh, and boys? Be thorough. Let her linger — she will make it clear when she has reached her limit.

Daytime Flirting!

Remember, folks, the whole game of sex is our imagination and our anticipation regarding our desires. Why wait to flirt only in the bedroom? If you want to spice things up, make an effort to flirt with each other all day long.

Shush the Bedroom Ambiance

Do away with a cluttered bedroom and make way for some candles. Use the silk sheets now and then. Warm up the room. Add some soft music. The more inviting the room, the sooner you'll be nestled in each other's arms... to say the least.

Add Sex Slots to the Calendar

It may seem boring to plan sex at first glance, but it can bring sex to a new level! Both partners have some time for grooming, buying a sexy outfit — whatever turns you two on. And don't just choose a date and time. Choose a place, a game you're going to play, a new position to try, and more.

CHAPTER 14:

Practice Empathy

Now that you understand a little more about empathy, you have to start communicating with it in mind. If you struggle with finding the right things to say, the following statements might help you figure it out.

Acknowledge Your Partner's Pain

You need to acknowledge how they feel at all times. They will feel supported when you connect with their struggle or pain.

You may use the following sentences:

- "I am sorry that you have to go through this."
- "I hate that this happened to you."
- "I wish I could turn things around and make it easier for you."
- "This must be hard for you."
- "I can see that this must be a difficult situation for you."

Share Your Feelings

You can be truthful and admit it when you don't know what to say or do. It is not always easy to imagine what the other person is going through. Share your thoughts and let your partner know that you are trying.

You may use the following sentences:

- "I wish I could make things better."
- "My heart hurts for you."
- "I can't imagine how hard this must be for you."
- "I'm unfortunate that this happened to you."
- "I'm sorry that you are feeling this way."

Show Your Partner that You Are Grateful When They Open Up to You

People find it challenging to open up and be vulnerable to others. More often than not, their trust has been broken at some point. So, when they choose to trust you, you need to be grateful and express it. Show your partner you appreciate that they share their thoughts and emotions with you. Acknowledge how difficult it can be for them to do this sometimes. You may use the following sentences:

- "I'm glad that you shared this with me."
- "I'm glad that you are telling me this."
- "I can imagine how hard it must be to talk about this. Thank you for sharing it with me."
- "I appreciate you trying to work hard on our relationship. I know you are trying, and that gives me hope."

- "Thank you for trusting me and opening up. I want to be there for you."

Show Your Partner that You Are Interested.

You have to take an interest in what your partner is going through. It can be hard to go through difficult times alone. You have to reach out and show them that you are there for support. Show them that you are interested in listening to whatever they have to say. Don't offer too much advice or too many opinions. Just be a good listener. You may use the following sentences:

- "I'm here for you if you want to talk."
- "How are you feeling about all that's been going on lately?"
- "Are you OK? Is there something you want to talk about?"
- "I think you're feeling like ____. Am I right? Did I misunderstand?"
- "What has this been like for you?"

Show Encouragement

When your loved one is going through a tough time, you have to be encouraging. But you need to go about this the right way. Don't try to fix their problem or offer unsolicited advice. Just encourage them in a way that makes them feel better and motivated. Show them that you care and that you believe in them.

414 | P a g .

You may use the following sentences:

- "You are strong, and I believe you can get through this."
- "I am always on your side. You should never feel alone."
- "I'm proud of everything that you have done."
- "You matter, and you should never question it."
- "You are a very talented person."

Show Support

Actions matter more than words at times. You can take some simple actions to show your partner you support and help them through tough times. You can send them flowers to make them feel better. You can do some chores for them. Just do anything that you feel they will appreciate, making their lives a little easier. You may use the following sentences:

- "I want to do this for you."
- "I am always here to listen."
- "Is there anything I can do for you right now?"
- "Is there any way I can help?"
- "Tell me what you need."

But in the end, there is no fixed script when it comes to sympathy. You have to be more attuned to your partner's needs and act likewise. Half the work is just listening and being there for them. I hope the examples given here help you deal with such situations better and more empathetic.

Conclusion

N ow, all that is left to do is get working on your relationship to ensure that it is as healthy as you would like it to be. Remember, the mindful relationship is one in which both parties can engage mindfully to recall what matters to them at the moment. It is one that will allow both parties to work together to focus on communicating honestly, calmly, and without judgment.

Mindfulness is the simple human capacity to be completely aware, know where we are and what we are doing, and not be too reactive or distracted by what's going on around us. It's not a woo-woo that you have to spend hours studying or flying to a distant land to discover. It's open to you and your partner right now.

The mindful relationship is one that will help you and your partner become the best couple you can be. It will help you to unlock your untapped potential. It will help you to figure out how to better process events that happen when they are stressed, or it can help you figure out how to solve conflicts.

Remember to make use of the varying activities designed to allow you and your partner to work together, or alongside each other, to allow you to be continuously dedicated and contribute to the betterment of your relationship. Over time, you will find that your bonds will strengthen. You will find that intimacy and love will burn brighter. Your relationship does not have to be perfect, but it should provide everything you are looking for if you and your partner are both committed to communicating fairly and respectfully

We are approached to tune in, be persistent, and comprehend our musings, propensities, and inclinations, so we may discover empathy for the pieces of ourselves that we dislike to such an extent. Dejection, outrage, dread, envy — they will, in general, exist in each one of us. Some have a hold on it; a few of us don't. Having a critical relationship relies upon our capacity to be distant from everyone else and with us. An insightful individual perceives that they are 'stick' to their accomplice out of a feeling of need.

Whether you have decided to begin implementing the activities or just work with the material provided for now, you will find that you are at a great advantage having access to insight to make your relationship better.

Remember to pay attention to the most common relationship conflicts that are out there. Ensure that you are not actively falling into the relationship, bad habits, or toxic tendencies mentioned. Keep in mind that you should put most of your focus on how to build up and nurture your relationship so that you know that it will be as useful and beneficial to you and your partner as possible. Relationships should be treated as a team with mindful respect toward each other as teammates. If you can do that, you and your partner will be able to take on the world. Good luck as you set out on your journey to bettering yourself. You and your partner can do it!

Made in the USA
Coppell, TX
08 December 2020

43699707R00233